THE WORKING WRITER

STAYING CREATIVE THROUGH THE SEASONS OF LIFE

GEETANJALI MUKHERJEE

*To the working writers who choose to stay creative, no matter the season.
To every writing mentor who has inspired me to keep going.
To my parents, who always support my dreams, even when they seem impractical and out of reach.*

INTRODUCTION

"It's hell writing and it's hell not writing. The only tolerable state is having just written."
  – **Robert Hass**

"Writing is like breathing, it's possible to learn to do it well, but the point is to do it no matter what."
  – **Julia Cameron**

I see a writer as someone who is writing all the time – whether or not they are actually sitting at their desk and putting words down. They write when they save interesting articles from the (digital) newspaper or order a stack of new books (despite their already overflowing bookshelves). They write when they are sitting in a bus or crowded café, eavesdropping on interesting conversations and taking notes in an app on their phone. They write when they say no to invitations from friends to stay home and write and end up spending the entire evening overhauling the outline *again* (without actually writing a single new word in the manuscript).

Writing is more than sitting in a café and typing on a laptop.

It's more than bestseller lists and book signings and adoring fans waiting in line for their favorite author's latest summer release. Most writers struggle with making the time to write, fighting against their own fears and wishing they could write like [insert big name writer here]. Writers are no different than everyone else, except they are more neurotic, read as if it's a competitive sport, and feel constantly guilty that they aren't writing 'enough', and then spend their writing window stalking successful writers on social media to see what kind of writing software they use or how they arrange their notebooks.

To me a *working writer* is someone who writes with dedication, on a semi-regular basis, whether they make their living from writing or not. I have a day job and am only able to write in small pockets of time. During busy periods at work, I might not get much actual writing done for weeks at a time, but I am always thinking of myself as a writer and thinking like a writer. I read books daily, usually during my commute (before the pandemic and era of work from home), sometimes during my lunch break or before bed. I also tried to write daily but found that a harder habit to maintain. Now I try to write as often as I can, but even when I am not putting words down on the page, I am doing research, writing outlines, taking notes on other books I might want to write. I write in my journal about the things I want to write, complain about my book sales and contemplate what might be stopping me from working on my current book. In short, I am a working writer every day, whether or not I produced *publishable* words that day.

This book is for working writers.

This book is a collection of essays edited from blog posts I wrote over the space of a few years, on creativity and the writing process. During the pandemic, I decided to compile some of the posts into a book, to include as part of a series of books on the writing process.

After work, I sat in the evenings to curate and edit the posts, trying to choose ones that might speak to a fellow writer. My hope for this book is that it will motivate writers who need inspiration to keep going, to keep coming back to the words, to the writing life. I wanted to reach writers who are managing many responsibilities and are perhaps wrestling with finding the time and inspiration to stay the course, to continue to show up despite the ups and downs of the writer's life.

Inexplicably, every blog post I decided to include seemed to have advice that was tailor-made for me. Whatever I was struggling with in my own writing life at the time, I found a mirror in the essays I was editing. I didn't remember writing those words, but I felt inspired by them. It was comforting to know that I had gone through similar struggles with my writing before and gotten through it then. Therefore, I told myself, I could get through it again.

I decided not to change the specific details of when and where I wrote the posts – which is why many of the essays reference books that I published a few years ago or writing challenges that I have already overcome. In fact, it gave me comfort to know that I had actually finished the book I was struggling with at the time and written many more after despite my now-busier schedule.

In these essays, I explore the challenges of finding time to write, breaking through writer's block, dealing with deadlocked projects and overcoming the fear of perfectionism, among other topics related to the writing and creative process.

I believe that a working writer is constantly learning and improving at different aspects of their craft, and as such I love to keep learning from writers of both fiction and non-fiction, via their books, blog posts and podcasts. Some of the essays in the book feature lessons I learned from other writers, as well as from well-regarded experts in the fields of psychology and neuroscience.

I compiled this book of essays on the writing life with the hope that it will inspire other writers to continue with this life, regardless of whether you're working on your first book or twentieth. The writing life, while it can bring particular moments of frustration, can also be incredibly fulfilling.

I hope that you are able to similarly take away something from the book to add to your own personal process or inspire you in whatever writing challenge you're currently facing.

1

WHERE DO YOU GET IDEAS FROM?

A lot of interviews with authors and other creative people feature this question – "Where do you get your ideas from?" It seems that many people would like to be more creative, would like to write books and screenplays, but suffer from a paucity of ideas, and feel that maybe there is some secret that successful authors are privy to that others are not.

There is no secret stash of ideas. And even if there were, it does not matter. Here's why.

Ideas are not the most important aspect of creation

Most people, me included, feel very excited when they get an idea – the first moments after a flash of inspiration are heady, when you feel on top of the world, you feel brilliant and invincible and like you got a glimpse into the heart of the universe.

The reality is, however, that getting the idea is the easy part. It is executing it that is hard, that takes tremendous discipline and perseverance and development of skill. Execution separates doers from wannabes, it separates the professionals from the amateurs. The real exercise of creativity lies in the daily toiling away at a project till it is as good as you can make it, and then sending it out into the world.

Ideas live in the confluence of diversity

Some people say that there are no original ideas, that we are simply reworking the same concepts over and over. I disagree, but it is true that being original can be difficult when it seems everything has been done to death.

There are two ways around this: firstly, being original comes, like writing coach Julia Cameron says, from being true to yourself, from delving into your own truth. What unique perspective do you have on the world? How do you see the same events, people, situations differently from those around you? How can you make what's familiar and every day to you seem fascinating and alive to someone else? For instance, Amy Tan grew up in a Chinese-American community where the stories of mothers and daughters clashing over cultural values was commonplace, but the rest of the world was fascinated with her portrayal of ordinary women and their stories.

Secondly, an original idea is often the surprising marriage of two unrelated ideas, something that no one thought to put together, but once they are, you wonder how no one thought of it before. Like ice-cream cake. Or putting technology and the ancient Greeks together, in the *Hunger Games* trilogy. You are more likely to come up with an interesting and original idea if you regularly dabble in completely different pursuits, hobbies and interests.

Capturing and accessing ideas is crucial

Having the best ideas in the world are of no use if you can't remember them, or can't find the piece of paper you scribbled your amazing idea down on. Ideas can come to you anywhere,

(I usually get them while walking), and it's important that you can jot them down and be able to find them again when you need them. There are several ways of capturing your ideas, and you can choose what works for you, as long as you are consistent.

Some people swear by the pen and paper method, and if you are so inclined, you could invest in a beautifully crafted journal (or a cheap one) and a pen that writes easily, and start jotting all your ideas in it. Just remember to keep it with you at all times.

For the more technologically minded, with dozens of smartphone apps, you are spoilt for choice with note-taking apps. I won't date this book by mentioning specific apps, as I am sure by the time you read this, there will be new ones (or our phones have become lenses attached to our glasses or something equally likely). If you really want to know what apps I use, read my blog or message me on social media.

The important thing isn't what app you use but that it is something that is easy for you to use, has the features you need and that you will use regularly. If you use a few different places to capture your ideas, just ensure that you take the time every week or so to copy your ideas over to one Master document or folder or notebook.

Generating ideas is really not that difficult when you realise that it is simply the first of a long series of steps towards that idea becoming a concrete product or being consumed or used in some way. When you take the pressure off, are willing to start small and start simple, and learn to listen for and retain ideas when they present themselves to you, you will soon be inundated with far more ideas that you can find use for.

Where do you get your ideas from? And more importantly, what do you do next?

2

AVOIDING THE RESEARCH TRAP

Creating something out of thin air can be nerve-wracking, and one of the ways we try to subconsciously avoid this is by doing what Cal Newport calls "pseudo-work". While he refers to this in the context of studying for tests, we creative professionals can recognize that this is akin to hiding behind the old excuse – "I need to do some more research".

Don't get me wrong - there is nothing wrong with doing research. I used to be an academic researcher, writing academic-style papers and books, and those were founded on solid research. However, precisely because research is so important in such projects, it is very difficult to know when enough is enough, and to stop doing research and get down to doing the actual *writing*. Even in non-academic fields, such as fiction writing, writers are sometimes tempted to read ever-more interesting, but irrelevant books on the types of wines served at the table of Swedish kings in the 18th century, when it is not really pertinent to the story at hand. Anything to avoid figuring out how the main characters actually get past the guards and escape in the fight scene in Chapter 8.

I was facing this problem while writing one of my non-fiction books. It was going very slowly, which was very frustrating at the time. When trying to brainstorm ways to move it along faster and figure out why it was stalling, I mapped out the time that I had spent on it so far. The book was actually an adaptation of my master's thesis, so theoretically I had already done the important research already. Why then was it still taking so long?

And then it hit me - I had spent a whole month or so working continuously on this project – during which time it should have significantly moved forward and got me far closer to finishing. Except that in that whole time - I did not write *a single word*. That's right - not one word. I did a lot of research - and I read through it all with highlighters - and I even copied out the relevant quotes. What I didn't do was add even a word of that to my manuscript. I did move paragraphs around - broke it up into chapters, reorganized it and moved the chapters around again. All that took a lot of time and I really thought I was working. Except it was pseudo-work - none of it got me any closer to a finished book.

I decided that I had to either complete this project or decide to let it go and move on to something else, because I couldn't keep spinning my wheels. Doggedly not wanting to let go, completion was my only option. And I started to work on adding new writing to the WIP.

To see how much I was actually getting done, I kept a simple table in a note in Evernote - with the starting and ending words of the day. It soon became a little game with myself - to add more words than the day before - although many days I only progressed a little bit. Sometimes that frustrated me - and I wished it would move much faster. Until I realized - even adding 500 more words that day was more than I had done when I was just doing research and nothing else. At least now I was writing - some of it might be edited out, but it was progress. I wasn't deluding myself about writing when I wasn't.

It's actually really easy to fall into the *research trap* without even realizing it. I kept having to ask myself if I really needed to add in any more research to the section I was working on. I know how easy it is to say, "But I must add in this one more fact, and then I must find that other report to corroborate it", and before I know it, I have lost several hours. At several points during the writing stage, I found myself chasing up obscure journal articles online, one after another, down research rabbit holes. As soon as I realized this - I set a time limit - that I would not spend more than two days on a section at most. Updating the table showing me clearly how much progress I was making (or not), and how many days I was spending on each section, kept me semi-accountable. Which is one of the main benefits of tracking such metrics, something I am learning the hard way.

Is there a project in which you are unwittingly falling into the research trap?

3

———

FIRST DRAFT IS KING

A few years ago, I wrote the script for a musical that was staged by a community organization that I have been volunteering with since I moved to Singapore. This was the first time I had done something like this, and I was nervous and excited in equal parts.

I actually didn't write the first draft of the script, someone else wrote a few initial scenes and placeholders for dances and songs that were composed by others. To be perfectly honest, the draft I saw didn't read too well - it felt very stiff and formal, the dialogue was stilted and the essence of the story, the emotions, weren't really coming across. I was brought in to make changes as I saw fit, which meant going over the entire script and making changes to everything other than the underlying structure.

Through this process I learnt so much about my own struggles to complete my writing projects. Although the first draft was quite flawed, having it in place saved us a ton of time. Having something to work on made me approach the work differently, with a lot more confidence and less pressure than I would otherwise have faced. I was able to break down the work in my mind into this set of lines, this scene, this speech. I worked on it a bit at a time, and the combination of reduced pressure from already having a draft and focusing on a few lines at a time helped to completely transform the script.

We made several small but important changes – making the dialogue more natural, adding in more strategic interaction between the characters and finding alternatives to work around the design elements. Through this process, I realized the fundamental importance of a completed first draft, no matter how terrible. I had read about the importance of the "shi**y first draft", but I just assumed that since they are written by great writers, their standards of really terrible would differ from mine, and there was no way I could write really badly and then improve it substantially. I assumed I would have to sort out the knotty design and structural problems, figure out where to add in the really important thematic points and have all my research done BEFORE I worked on the first draft because these were substantive issues. This experience taught me that drafts can be completely transformed just by changing a few things, and the work feels much more doable when layered onto an existing, completed document.

Hence, lesson learned – first draft is really king, and anything can be achieved ONCE the first draft is in place.

So what project are you putting off till you have all the elements in place, where you can start right now with a baseline first draft?

4

____

FIRST IMPRESSIONS MATTER

*R*ecently I have been reading a bunch of books for review - going through the backlog of books I promised to review as well as reading a few ARCs (advanced reader copies) of books that I would have read anyway, provided by the publisher. And one thing I found with the ARCs was the negative impression most of them made because of relatively minor issues that are easily fixed - poor formatting and typos.

To be clear, I am not talking about the occasional misplaced comma or an extra page lurking in the manuscript. I mean that for at least two of the books I had difficulty reading even a paragraph because the formatting at least on my copy of the book was terrible. There were no page or chapter breaks, or sentences abruptly had entire line spaces in the middle. It was as if an eight-year old had done the formatting. Actually, it might be insulting to that eight-year old, who might actually have done a better job. Several of the books also had many glaring typos and errors. I stopped keeping track after the 20th typo. While it is likely that many of these mistakes will be corrected before the book goes to print, it is possible that many of them will remain in the manuscript. And since the books in question are by big-name authors, the mistakes will be ignored by readers, and may not affect the fate of the book or the message in any way.

However, as an indie author, I am acutely aware that there is a glaring double-standard - what Random House or Simon & Schuster can get away with, you or I as an indie cannot. The other day I was on a Facebook group for authors, where one debut author asked why her book wasn't selling or being read on Kindle Unlimited (an Amazon program that allows readers to read essentially an unlimited number of books every month), despite the price of the book being $0.99. And while I didn't click through to her book, many others had, and the primary comment was that of a poor impression being made - a less-than stellar cover and too many errors in the sample.

Quite often authors write to me to request an interview for my blog, and I have had occasion to look at the books and Amazon profiles of many indie authors. Something that always amazes me is the number of times I find glaring errors or terrible grammar in book descriptions. If I can't get through a 200-word description because of a poor writing style, I won't exactly be enticed into reading the book. And the flip side happens as well - I have been excited about a book simply from reading the description, sometimes just the first line. I don't read a lot of YA or young adult novels for instance, but the first sentence of the back cover blurb of the Red Queen series got me hooked - I didn't need to read more to know I would enjoy the books.

All of this is to say, that as an indie author, the odds often seem stacked against us. I know that we are all doing our best, having taken on the duties covered traditionally by publishers, and it can seem like a lot. But before railing against Amazon or readers or wondering why your sales are abysmal - take a fresh look at the impression your book is making. You don't need to spend thousands of dollars getting the best cover or the most credentialed developmental editor; but at the very least make sure your cover fits the expectations of the genre, and that your book is relatively error-free. Invest in a good copy-edit. Get your friends to look over your book description and see whether it pops or is underwhelming.

Each aspect of getting our work out there is almost a skill in itself. Joanna Penn talks about how she learnt to write good book descriptions by studying those of bestsellers in her genres. There is so much to learn it can be overwhelming. I have lists of things to do that include "re-write book descriptions" and research book categories and keywords. As we keep learning more, we need to revisit our books and apply that knowledge. We can't get it perfect every time, but there is a sense of satisfaction in knowing that we are taking action and making our books the best they can be.

None of these are guarantees that you will sell more, but there are enough barriers to discoverability as it is. Don't make it unnecessarily harder for yourself by letting your book make a poor first impression.

5

HOW DO YOU MAKE TIME TO WRITE?

I was answering questions for a couple of interviews about my writing and books recently, and one of the questions concerned finding time to write. And this got me thinking, how does one make time to write when everyone else makes demands on your time that are seemingly more urgent?

The beginning of a new year is a good time to ask these sort of big-picture questions. Anyone who is juggling multiple priorities will be wondering if they really have time to devote to writing or painting or setting up a side-business. Or you may already be making some time for this passion on the side, but you are frustrated that you are not able to spend enough time on it, enough time to really hone your skills, or take on an ambitious project that will give you a lot of traction. In that scenario, the sensible voice inside your head tells you to shelve your project till you have more time later.

Reading Laura Vanderkam's books on time management, I realized that we actually have a lot more free time than we realize, or rather time that is not being used by working and sleeping, that we can allocate how we choose. The problem is that most of us use a lot of that time inefficiently. Sometimes we take on chores or commitments that don't reflect our values, we do things that we don't really need to or want to and give up on things that are more important to us, because "we don't have enough time". At other times, we aren't conscious of how we are using our time, and before we know it, three hours have passed in watching mindless TV that wasn't even that important in the first place, or an hour has disappeared into "catching up with friends" on social media, even though we didn't exactly send any personal messages. What could we accomplish with just 3-4 hours every week devoted to our passion projects?

One thing I have been experimenting with this week is scheduling what's important to me first, and then worrying about everything else. This is similar to Stephen Covey's mantra of putting "first things first"– I found that things that I want to do and naturally used to say 'no' to before thinking I didn't have time for it, I can very often make time for. I just have to be more mindful of how I am using my time. I also have to be more willing to let the dishes pile up in the sink, and ignore the siren call of the laundry or the unread newsletters in my email. I won't really suffer if any of those things aren't done <u>right</u> now, and devoting half an hour instead to my current WIP, or taking the time to find new ways to market my books which could yield more sales is more satisfying and ultimately a better use of my time.

I also found strangely that the chores were still getting done; I was just getting through them faster, or perhaps batching them made it more efficient. Regardless, deciding how I was going to use my time, rather than just going about on autopilot, just doing what I always did before, actually helped me to find more time.

Ten Minutes a Day

I recently attended a gathering of a few friends celebrating one of my friends' acceptance to university. During our general catch-up, we discussed something that comes up regularly in conversations now – "I'm so busy", "I can't keep up with all my obligations". This is really common now in this always-on, digital age. But I think it's a more complicated problem for creative people.

I find that the list of creative projects that I want to get to is ever-increasing. And yet the pile of projects that I actually complete is ever-dwindling. This is incredibly frustrating to me, even more so because I dedicated this year to being more productive and accomplishing a lot more, partly by researching ways to harness technology and psychology to getting more done. Despite this, I find some weeks are a struggle just to get the urgent tasks done, and I can't seem to make time for my larger creative projects.

This morning, after days of feeling guilty about not doing any exercise and basically feeling terrible, I decided to spend one minute doing some yoga. I am not a yoga expert, in fact I have attended, over the course of a couple of years, maybe 15-20 classes in total. Depending on my current fitness level, I can do most beginner poses with ease, but pack too many of them into a one-hour session, and I will be looking desperately at the clock, willing it to move faster.

This background is to establish my credentials as someone who is generally unfit and not great at yoga. In fact, this morning, all I could remember was about 4 and a half poses, that I executed clumsily. Even so, that minute or 90 seconds of yoga instantly eliminated my aches and pains and feeling of stiffness, and I felt loads better. And instead of feeling guilty about not doing anything, I started to look forward to the next mini session.

Now I know that ten or less minutes of yoga a day isn't going to make me the most fit person around, but it is a great start. And it is much easier to convince yourself to do ten minutes of something, even when you're busy or tired or uninspired.

I read recently in *Tools of Titans* by Tim Ferriss about a meditation teacher who recommends that you take just one mindful breath a day. It's the same concept. Anyone can take one breath. It's not that hard.

So what does yoga and mindfulness have to do with creativity and writing? I think the same principle can be applied to being more creative. I know many people who say they would like to write a book, or do something creative that requires a large commitment of time. On hearing that I have written books, people invariably say, "I would love to write a book, *if only I had the time*". It's true that I have been fortunate enough to have had large chunks of time that I could devote to writing some of my books. But that wasn't the case for the first three books I published, and it certainly wasn't the case for several of my most recent books.

In fact, one of my books was several months behind schedule and got derailed several times because of external issues out of my control. I raced to finish it while I was juggling starting a new job in a completely new industry, settling into a new (old) city and dealing with health issues. The way I finally finished it - a few minutes of writing a day.

I often had only 10-15 minutes of time after my long commute home, and many days I would tell myself – "I'm too tired", or "I will get to it tomorrow". I thought I wasn't inspired, or that I needed to not be falling asleep with exhaustion in order to write. And the days went by, the end of the year got closer, and I was no nearer to finishing the book.

I was starting to panic, because I had imposed a deadline of publishing the book within the year. It had already been delayed enough, and I didn't want to delay it any further.

So I started working on it for ten minutes at a time. Some days I spent the time editing an essay on my morning commute. I carried my personal laptop with me, and found I could edit a few paragraphs each way. On other days I came home and spent a few minutes editing before dinner.

Progress was slow - most of the time I despaired that I was not any closer to finishing, because I was only working on a few paragraphs at a time. But one at a time I finished editing eight, then nine, then 11 essays. I had three essays left and about ten days before I would have to submit the book to be in time to publish it in December. I figured I could handle it, and get the work in on time.

And then I realized I had two important work projects due on Monday, and I would have to work over the weekend to get it done in time. And I had planned to complete the essays that weekend as well.

I panicked, then determined that I would work on all of the projects. I got my work assignments and the essays edited. In 15 minute increments. In between my work projects, I edited the essays, putting in 15 minutes on them before going back to my work assignments. Over the course of that weekend, I made substantial headway on my projects, which ultimately got handed in on time. And I completed my book.

I realize that everyone's life circumstances are different, and sometimes it just isn't possible to squeeze anything else in. This experience made me realize however, that I don't know how much more I am capable of accomplishing until I am pushed, until I have no choice but to challenge my assumptions of what I can and can't do.

And that's why I have set a big challenge for myself for next year - to write much more than I have so far, and to really stretch my capacity. If I can achieve it, it would be amazing and help my expand my writing abilities. If I can't, I probably would still get more writing done than I have before, and learn a lot from the attempt. So I win no matter what.

If you're reading this at the end of December / beginning of January (or at any time really), I encourage you to set a challenge for yourself that seems like a big stretch, something that makes you feel excited and nervous in equal measure. Share your goal or keep it to yourself, but don't hold back. After all, you will win either way.

Do you feel that you have enough time to devote to writing?

6

ALLOCATING TIME AND
CHOOSING PROJECTS

I am working on revising a book I published in 2014. It is taking far longer than I would have liked, and at least every couple of days I ask myself if it is worth it. It is common to issue revised editions of books from traditionally published authors, at least for non-fiction, which is the genre my book is in as well. But as a self-published author, it may not really make a lot of commercial sense to spend time writing something that I have already published, especially when there is often a lot of pressure to publish new books consistently and often.

The book in question is based on my Master's thesis, and has already been revised once - when I was first converting it to a book. At the time the book was initially published, I was new to being an author, and had a lot to learn. Although I am proud of the research I did and my conclusions, the book itself needed work. As I read more non-fiction, as well as books on craft, I realized that if I wanted to reach a wider audience, I would need to revise the book and make it more accessible.

Sometime last year I took a closer look at the book and revised the structure to make it flow better, and to combine some ideas that were spread around the book, and break up others that were clumped together. It was a difficult process because this was so new to me and I was grappling with such new skills, but when the pieces finally clicked into place, I was reminded exactly why I love writing - for the feeling of solving a difficult jigsaw puzzle.

Unfortunately, it has since taken me months to get going on the revision - partly because there were other important projects in the way. It was hard to justify the time spent on an old book when new ones, some half-written, beckoned. Also, a lot of the time, spending time on commercial projects or focusing on marketing and sales seemed more pragmatic than reworking something that may not lead to any justifiable commercial or concrete gains. This sort of thinking is inevitable for a working creative who has multiple demands on their time, but to be honest I hated thinking of my work in that way. I think of myself as an artist, and surely spending the time to improve my art would be worth my time? Or if I wanted to reframe it more pragmatically, surely honing my skills as a writer would result in better future books?

Given that I am writing a book on being a working writer, it can be tempting to hide any aspect of the process that show-cases doubts, or that impacts in any way my authority as a creative professional. However, one of the main reasons I wanted to write this book was to provide insight into the life of a working writer, and hopefully illustrate that one rarely has all the answers – it is usually a process of doing what makes sense at the time and hoping that you made the right decision. It is hard to admit to doubts, missteps or creative failures publicly. It is easier to claim that each project was perfect from the start, that each phase was effortless and that one's creative success was an inevitable consequence of one's creative genius. That is certainly not the case for me, and I like to think that it isn't the case for most other creatives as well.

In the world of software, iteration is a common concept. You start with something, and you keep working on it, adding, tinkering, till it gets much better. Sometimes, quite often, you put it out as a product or a feature, and keep improving it and working on it. As an indie author, I think that should be closer to our style of working - do the best you can the first time, but keep working on improving your skills and if you think something needs re-working, don't be afraid to come back to it later. I know many authors periodically refresh their covers and book descriptions, but I think we shouldn't be afraid to do more than that if warranted.

Back to my book - I did complete the revision and publish the second edition. It took a while to get back into the rhythm of the book, as I had spent so much time away from it. I remembered how much I enjoyed researching and writing this book, and sometimes it was a challenge to stop myself from wanting to get lost again in that research, instead of doing only what was absolutely needed to revise it efficiently.

Solo entrepreneurs and indie authors share in common a specific struggle - knowing what to prioritize. Having a boss can be annoying, but the upside is that someone decides for you what to work on, and what not to bother with. I don't have that problem (or benefit) when it comes to my writing, and need to decide for myself what is and isn't worth my time. Given that time is always the one thing all of us need more of, it is tough to know sometimes how to allocate it. The rule of thumb for me I found, is that I don't regret spending time on projects that take my skill and craft forward and help me to become a better writer.

How do you decide how to allocate your creative time?

7

MAKING A BIG DEAL
OF YOUR WRITING

As writers we love to romanticize experiences, particularly the act of writing. As is quite common for me, over the past year, I have been battling many of these romantic notions and myths within myself. One of which was that I convinced myself that I had to have a huge chunk of time in which to write.

If I had only 20 minutes before I had to get up to make dinner, I told myself that it wasn't enough time to get anything written. If I had a lot of work to do that day, then I would convince myself that I had no time to write, feel huffy and annoyed, and take many breaks which involved some combination of scrolling through social media, watching TV and playing Candy Crush on my phone. But that didn't count because I couldn't write knowing how much work I had to do, could I?

The other myth that I insidiously incorporated was the ever so common, "I have to wait till I am inspired". I have read so many books and articles on this one, with productive and successful writers simply scoffing at the writer who believes that they need to be inspired first. Hah, who ever heard of such a thing! But the thing was, these writers simply said what not to do – don't wait for inspiration, don't be a ninny.

They never tell you what to do instead - when you're sitting there staring at the screen, when finally there are no other distractions and you've got your special writing hat on, and your mind is blank. Completely. Other than the fact that you're panicking slightly because you thought that when you did finally sit down to write and there was time and space to think, you would have, you know, writerly thoughts. Not "oh gosh I can't think of anything to say. Maybe I am not meant to be a writer after all". Then you wade into dangerous territory, and far from putting any words down, you start to question this whole "being a writer" aspiration.

Since I struggle with these kinds of things all the time, I am not really equipped to "give advice and tell you what to do". I will share however, what I have been doing, and hope that helps somewhat.

One of my favorite writing books, and the book that finally got me writing somewhat regularly, is Julia Cameron's *The Right to Write*. I think this book should be required reading for anyone who wants to put words down with any regularity. In this book, Cameron tells us over and over that writing shouldn't be made into a big deal. We don't need some special tools, or the perfect circumstances to write. We just need to do it, much like the Nike slogan.

Throughout her book, she gives advice on how to actually do this - keep a notebook with you and just jot down some thoughts. Make the writing easy, light. Put in things around you, things that are happening to you, put in everything that's on your mind and keeping you from your writing.

This brings to mind a saying that is attributed to Nora Ephron: "Everything is copy". No matter what is going on in your life, big or small, put it in your writing. And this is exactly what Julia does in her own work, and it works. She writes about meeting a friend for coffee, about strolling through Central Park, about feeding her horses. And as she writes about these seemingly mundane details, she teaches you how to turn the mundane details of your own life into something meaningful, something creative.

All of us have distractions and obligations that get in the way of our writing. Instead of railing against them, maybe we simply need to work with them and incorporate them into our writing schedule.

Today was a perfect example. I started this piece soon after waking in the morning, with a cup of coffee. Then I got distracted, and decided I may as well start my day, do the things I needed to. By the time I got down to doing work, I got distracted again with a phone call, and was despairing of ever getting back on my long list of to-dos. And to be completely honest, I was a little annoyed. The day seemed to be getting away from me, I hadn't really done much writing and not much else. And I had to catch up, because yesterday was a public holiday, and I didn't get much done because I decided to use the opportunity to clean the house (which it really needed, since I usually swap out cleaning time for writing or reading). Anyway, I told myself that I wasn't in the mood to write, since I was annoyed and delayed and I had so much to do, if only I could figure out where to start.

Have you had a day like this? You designated some time to write, really got yourself going in your head, planning what you would work on, imagining how much you would get done, getting your cup of tea or coffee and just beginning to start when something interrupted you. By the time you got back to it - whether 5 or 50 minutes later, somehow it wasn't the same. No longer feeling all calm and rested, now you're anxious because you don't have much time left, and you haven't done what you needed to, and you're thinking, why bother even starting now - I couldn't possibly get anything done with this little bit of time.

This was me. Basically, all the time. I would get my writing done, yes, but it was excruciating. I had all these rules - I need so much time, I need to be in this frame of mind, I need my cup of coffee, and so on. It's almost a miracle I got any writing done at all. Well actually, I did it by keeping people at bay, by feeling guilty about every minute I wasn't writing, and then feeling anxious when I was actually at the keyboard, typing.

All this is because I made such a big deal of my writing. I read all about sh*tty first drafts and allowing yourself to write many drafts and tried every trick in the book. But I still felt like every word was a performance in front of a very judgmental crowd, and that I was failing spectacularly. I was stilted and formal and pushed aside the thoughts that did come into my head as not appropriate, not correct enough.

The more I write though, and the more I remind myself of the need to just do it, and not to think so much, it gets easier. I let more of my personality into the page. I leave my first thoughts alone, because they are usually more honest, more authentic, more me. I need to edit less, and let the ideas flow more.

Last night, I was cooking dinner in tandem with my dad. I started a dish, but he wanted to take over the kitchen, so I did some of my prep and left him to it. I knew he would probably be done in around 20 minutes or so, and in the past, I would have felt annoyed because it was too little time to do any "real" writing or get into serious work, and so I would have just played a game or tried to read. But somehow my defenses were down, and I thought I would just open Scrivener and have a little fun - write a few words and see what happened. And I managed to write 1,300 words of a new essay for my current work-in-progress. And that's 1,300 words more than I would have had if I had waited for the perfect opportunity or made a big deal of my writing.

This is not really an easy lesson to learn, and I don't think I have truly learnt it myself yet. I have days like yesterday, when I manage to effortlessly (or so it seemed) put the words down in between doing other things. And then I have a day like I did just the other day, when I took my laptop to a café to write, but between the kids screaming for red velvet cake and the businessmen making deals on their cellphones, I found it hard to concentrate. I did get some words down, but every word felt like I had to carve it on a tablet, and after struggling mightily to eke out less than a thousand words, I gave up, packed up my things and came home.

The lesson I suppose is that if you can get into the habit of just dropping some words in here and there, in between other things, then when you have a little larger chunk of time, you will be better equipped to use it well. And if you can't find any large chunks, well, at least you still have those ten minutes while waiting for the coffee to percolate.

In what ways are you making a big deal of your writing?

8

————

**DEALING WITH A
DEADLOCK IN MY WIP**

I have recently been having trouble with finishing one of my book projects. The problem was that I was done with two-thirds of the book, and I was stuck on the last third. But this section is important, because it includes both the introduction and the conclusion. This is a non-fiction book, and it's a project that I have had a lot of trouble with so far, probably because it's one of my most ambitious till date.

Anyway, I don't want to bore you with details about why exactly I was stuck or what was going wrong with the book. Suffice it to say, I had no ideas, I felt that everything I had already written wasn't good enough, but I didn't have any better ideas. Basically I was scared. I was scared that all my hard work over months on the parts that I had already written would be wasted. I was struggling with deciding how to begin the book, which sets the tone for the rest of it.

And this was probably the reason I was stuck. I was scared of getting it wrong, and I had made it all too important. Each of the chapters I was stuck on was *really important*, and I was in danger of messing them up big time.

I even stopped working on the book. I found plenty of

excuses, there were other things to do, other books to write, promotion stuff to do - basically I was busy. I didn't have time to worry about this book.

But I did. That's all I worried about some days. It was always on my mind, and the problem got bigger and bigger. I couldn't see a way out. I was doing that one thing we have been told not to do over and over - wait for inspiration.

So I decided to tackle it head on. As I keep advising others to do when tackling a thorny project, I began with the smallest, easiest part of the easiest chapter. And I tried to lower my mental standards as much as possible, stared down the fear (or the "Resistance" as Steven Pressfield calls it) and just made progress an inch at a time. I added a sentence here. I did some research and found something to rethink there. The more time I spent with it, I realized I could re-arrange one of the sections in that chapter, moving things around.

And as I worked on it, I stumbled upon inspiration. A book I was reading on innovation, completely unrelated to the topic of my book, or so I thought, gave me ideas for some additional research to include. Another book I was listening to, on trading and Wall Street, again a totally unrelated subject, helped me to see a way of structuring my introduction. I found the story I wanted to open a chapter with. I came across the facts I needed to fill in the gaps in the unredeemable middle chapter, which is now shaping up nicely.

The whole time I fretted and waited for the book to get better, waited for some miraculous way out of my deadlock, I had nothing. But when I decided to work on it anyway, to just tweak whatever I could, to get into the trenches and fight my way out of the mud, I started to see the light. On my book, and in general, about my writing.

Some days it feels like the book is this ugly, perverse thing that refuses to comply, that refuses to do my bidding. But then I realize, it's not the book, it's the fear about the book. The Resistance. If only I had recognized this sooner, I could have saved myself time and hassle. But maybe this is all part of the writing process. Each lesson building on the other. Like Hemingway said, this is a craft at which none of us ever become masters. All we can hope to do is get into the ring and go one more round with Resistance.

What do you do when you're stuck on an ongoing project?

9

THE SHADOW OF PERFECTIONISM

I have been busy trying to complete a new book that I really thought would be done by now - especially as the first draft of this book only took me three weeks to write, which is quite a record for me.

However, the subsequent drafts are taking more than twice as long, which is very frustrating. I have been racking my brains trying to figure out why. I'm putting in more hours than I did before (in fact, I meticulously track my writing time every day, so I know how much my time commitment has increased by). I am working on the book every day, reducing time spent on errands and socializing so that I can make faster progress.

The other thing I have done much better with this book than previous ones is to track my progress, and plan what I will get done, how and when. I have steps laid out that describe what I will do in what order, and then I also write daily goals. The problem is that I never seem to be able to complete what I plan to each day, and even when I do, it feels like I'm going at a very slow pace.

The only explanation for the slow progress - perfectionism. I have been laboring over every footnote, every reference, every sentence. Even though my planning process provides for a line editing stage later, once the content has been finalized, since there is no point perfecting a sentence that ultimately gets thrown out. And yet, I can't seem to stop myself from editing line by line anyway.

I have been trying to apply the advice from writing coach Hillary Rettig, who in her book *The 7 Secrets of the Prolific* suggests not worrying about trying to perfect anything while working on a piece of writing. Her approach - just make simple, doable changes and edits and move on to the next section, and by doing things just in little bits, she assures you that you actually make faster progress, with less stress. Somehow that approach isn't working - because I can't seem to leave a section till the thorny problems are worked out. And that tendency makes me avoid sections - because I know it has thorny problems that I will then be forced to fix, right then and there.

This is where the title of this post comes in: the shadow cast by perfectionism. By insisting my work looks perfect as I go along, or that I do research again on sections that I have already written, I am going much slower than I need to, feeling frustrated and hating the process of writing a book that initially I was really looking forward to. Not only that, since I have been thinking about perfectionism, I have been seeing how it has been rearing its ugly head almost everywhere in my life lately.

I put off writing blog posts because I don't feel I have the perfect topic to write about. Or start working on my novel - which till just a little while ago I was quite excited about. Or a long list of other things. There are so many projects that I won't even begin because I am worried that I won't do them perfectly.

I know many readers (perhaps coming from the same place I usually am) think perfectionism is a good thing, that it just another name for "having standards". Sure, it is good to have standards. But what if they hold you back from achieving what you really want to in life? Lately, I have been really thinking about what I want to accomplish, and realized that time is an incredibly finite resource that is slowly ticking away whether we are making the best use of it or not.

Recently, I read about some incredibly successful women, mostly my own age, who have accomplished a lot, in fields they knew nothing about when they started. This made me think - what would I be able to accomplish if I were to stop demanding to do it perfectly? This question has been bringing up some uncomfortable answers. It appears there is a lot I could do if I weren't hung up on doing everything perfectly. Putting aside the fact that I haven't done anything perfectly ever (because how could you really, when everything is improvable), I think it is an impossibly high standard and one that would only allow you to try things you are already good at. And in my opinion that's no way to live. I would never grow or learn new things in that way. Or would learn very very slowly.

And really, that's the shadow of perfectionism. It stops you from being all you could be.

Ask yourself this question - *what would I be able to accomplish if I were to stop demanding to do it perfectly?*

Perfectionism as the Enemy of Productivity

Sometimes what we think of as lack of productivity can really be an attack of perfectionism. When I find myself not making progress, or as much progress as I would like, I always resort to comparing myself to others who are far more prolific, or labelling myself lazy. Rettig's book on perfectionism in writing made me realize that often my stalling progress can be linked back to too high standards on my part, and fear that I won't be able to meet those standards. In her book, Rettig describes the signs of a perfectionist attitude, and I recognized many of them in myself. She also describes a process for getting through writing a book, which I think can be applied to other projects as well.

I have a tendency to think as a writer that I should write one ok first draft, one much better second draft, and one final, well-polished third draft. Rettig dismisses this theory, and states that we should go through "as many drafts as it takes". Her advice: write a terrible first draft, make the next one slightly less terrible, and so on, until you are happy with the outcome. This approach basically allows you to suspend the anxiety associated with approaching your project, and you find yourself getting closer to the finished product much quicker, thanks to reduced procrastination and fear. For each draft she suggests tackling the obvious flaws, and moving on, which is similar to dealing with the low-hanging fruit first, one of my favorite approaches to difficult projects.

This concept reminded me of a concept in computer programming known as *iterating*. In the context of programming, you basically repeat a part of a program on a loop, till you get the desired result. In the context of work, it means to do a specific step in your workflow over and over, each time improving it slightly, getting it closer to the outcome you want. App developers do this all the time by releasing updates to their app over time, each version fixing a few more bugs, adding a few more features.

Perfectionism can permeate all aspects of your life

I have written about perfectionism a lot, and I thought I knew how it affected me and that it was a tendency I had to guard against. However, I didn't realize exactly how much it was affecting almost every aspect of my life. Probably I still don't.

Lately, I have been feeling a bit overwhelmed with all the things I need to do. I am fortunate, I have a lot of projects going on right now, many of them with other people, all of them work

I am excited about, or least I was initially. But right now, the number of obligations on my plate have grown beyond the point that I feel I can handle, and I am feeling the pressure.

Part of the problem is that I said yes to too many things and many of them are either coming due too close to each other, or have just been put off for too long and I feel guilty not completing them. I made lists and looked and re-looked and tried to get things off my plate - but unless I was willing to go back to people and say "Sorry, I took on too much and can no longer do this", I didn't know how to get it all done. And that's not really an option.

So the solution in my mind became I will do it all, just work harder and faster and feel more stressed till it is all done. Not a great idea, right?

But it seemed to me like I had no choice.

Until a few days ago, when I was meditating and I had a lightbulb moment – that maybe I was approaching this all wrong. Maybe I can do it all without losing my sanity - by letting down my standards to some extent. Now I am **not** suggesting I phone it in, I am suggesting that I ask myself what is the reasonable standard that this task requires and then do it.

For many things, when someone asks me to do something, I immediately decide it will be done the best way possible in the world. Even if they ask me to do A, I tack on B through E tasks. And then do them at 120% level. Now this was always appreciated, but it meant I did everything very slowly and couldn't complete as many projects. I started to think that I was either lazy or inefficient, and searched through the productivity literature for ways I could improve my productivity, increase efficiency and cut down on procrastination.

I did all that. But it never occurred to me that one of the biggest things holding me back and causing my productivity to plummet wasn't the fact that I was lazy or procrastinated too much, but that I was a perfectionist about every little aspect of every project. And that meant that sometimes I avoided working on something because it wasn't up to my impossible standards and I didn't know what to do about it. Or that I avoided taking on anything that was too challenging - for fear that I couldn't do it (read: couldn't do it excellently). Or that I added on unnecessary elements to tasks that didn't need them, and added time and effort that could be spent elsewhere.

This finally dawned on me this week, and I realized that I would need to go through my list and see where my need to do something perfectly was holding me up.

The thing with perfectionism, at least for me, is that while it's one thing to acknowledge that I have this problem and need to guard against it, it is another to see exactly what aspects of the project I am being perfectionistic about, and what is just me doing a good job or being conscientious.

For instance, I helped my mom publish a cookbook of family recipes. My role was mainly to edit and proofread the book, format the document and take photos. But I spent months on this project, trying to get every aspect to be completely flawless. Most publishers today, whether established or new, have a completely different model, and they can't afford to spend months perfecting every font and use of punctuation. I know that my mom wants me to do an ok job, and move on to other things. A wrong comma or a few extra spaces or a missed italic doesn't bother her very much. But no matter how hard I tried, I couldn't stop myself from wanting to spend several weeks perfecting the project, making sure there were absolutely no errors to be found.

The same obsessiveness has been making several other projects take much longer than it should to complete, or in some cases, even get off the ground. I was offered a wonderful opportunity to work with someone on a project that I have very little knowledge in. I was very excited, but then since they gave me leeway in the timeline, I decided I must read every possible book on the topic and become a subject expert. I did this because I felt that was the only way I could even begin to know how to approach the project. But it was only recently that I realized that I was asked to do this not because of my subject matter expertise, but my ability as a writer. I don't need to know everything possible on the topic. I don't need to spend months on background reading. I need to know enough to understand conversations and then trust my co-author who is the expert on this subject. I was using the need to know a perfect amount of information to deal with the anxiety I felt about beginning the project.

I hope by writing this that someone reading it recognizes similar tendencies in themselves, and realizes that if they are slow to complete projects it's not because they are lazy or somehow unmotivated. I know writing this clarified for me what specifically my perfectionism is about. Usually, for me, it is about not knowing how to begin, or wanting to be able to control the outcome. Getting a handle on my perfectionism can have a huge effect on my productivity, and yours too if this is something you struggle with. Before chasing off to read about tomato timers and caffeine pills, see if changing the parameters of your project and how you are approaching it makes a difference to your productivity levels. It sure did for me.

Much Ado About Writer's Block

Much has been written about writer's block. In fact, I have spent countless hours seeking out books and searching online for ideas that will help me to beat it. Over time, I have realized that writer's block is really another name for perfectionism. You can't put anything down on paper, or type anything on the screen, because everything you can think of to say sounds wrong even before you've written it. The longer you sit in front of the blank page or screen in front of you, the harder it gets to put something down, and eventually, you just get up in frustration, telling yourself that you are blocked.

Incidentally, I am a master at writer's block. I spent years planning the first chapter of a memoir that I wanted to write. This was going to be my first book, my most important book. If I didn't nail the first scene, then the book wouldn't come together. I never thought of writing the chapters I did know how to write, and simply putting the initial chapter in place later. Eventually, of course, I did employ that approach, in writing other books; but because of that thinking I lost years of writing time.

Perfectionism in writing is an insidious thing. It creeps up in the guise of "standards". Who wouldn't want to write well? Or ensure that they do a good job?

But there is a difference between having standards and perfectionism. Having standards implies that you care about quality, maybe you go over your work one more time, you take extra care while editing, you strive harder to get better as a writer. Perfectionism tells you that you have to get it right in one draft. There is no room for improvement, no room for error. With that attitude, no wonder we freeze up when faced with the prospect of having to write a first sentence. We stare at the blank page, aware of the importance of that first sentence and think – "This has to grab the reader. This has to be witty and entertaining and shed light into the mysteries of life". No wonder we are paralyzed.

How do you get away from perfectionism? You remind yourself that what you're working on is just a draft. I had a law professor who introduced our class to the concept of the *zero draft*. This is the stage even before the first draft, where you just put some thoughts down, noodle with ideas and directions in which to angle the essay. Even though the term first draft has the word "draft" in it, most people including myself, associate it with the final or near-final version of something. The same connotation weirdly doesn't apply to zero drafts. Starting with a zero draft gives you permission to write an unpolished, messy draft. Ever since I first learned about the concept, I always started my academic papers, and later my books, with a zero draft.

Which hasn't stopped me from needing several other drafts as well. When asked how many drafts a piece of writing might need, writing coach Hilary Rettig said, "As many as it takes".

I think the best way to combat the tendency towards perfectionism in your writing is to give yourself permission - permission to write something that needs to be edited. Permission to write something that isn't quite finished yet. And permission to write and publish something that isn't perfect, but is something better - it represents you.

Do you struggle with perfectionism in your creative work?

10

____

ON CULTIVATING PATIENCE

*L*ately, I finally have a bit more time to write, and yet have been feeling a little frustrated, because for some reason the words aren't flowing and it feels like I'm dragging my boots through treacle. When this happens, I find myself staring at the screen, or trying to think of what I was about to say as the words dry up in my head, or I start to type something and it feels like I have forgotten how to structure sentences.

Creativity coach Julia Cameron writes that this is "chop" - when your work starts to fall apart and it feels like you cannot proceed even one more inch. Apparently this period of struggle is necessary, and when you get through the other side, you are somehow a better writer: your work is more polished, different. It's good to know that I'm not alone in feeling like this, that perhaps this is normal. It's even tempting to think - oh, at the end of this period I will be a better writer! Maybe I should be grateful for this upheaval in my writing process.

Except I'm not. I feel like a pouty child who stamps her foot and says "I don't like this! I want this feeling to go away!" I'm not sure that I want to be one level better. I want to instead just be back to where I was - so that I can use this rare time I have to race through my work, and get at least a full draft of my current book done.

And this is where Julia warns us, that artists need to learn patience. That fun as it would be to race through the draft, perhaps what I need to learn is to take it slower - to allow the work to find its own rhythm. This is probably what is hardest for me - when the work is hard, or when I look at my abandoned drafts or the major revisions I have planned – that's when I wish I could click my fingers and find myself at the other side with a completed draft. I could then look at the work and say, yes it's really good. I can be assured of the quality of my work, and that I am on the right path.

And that's why patience is hard. I want results right now, because I am anxious. What if I am not a "real" writer? If I could only complete this manuscript, and I could be assured that it would do really well, then I would feel secure in my ability and my writerliness (yes, I made up that word; I'm a writer and I can do that!). So impatience really isn't my problem. It is about needing approval and validation.

Julia always says – "What if everyone were capable of being creative? What if there were no such labels?" I don't know if I can quite get my head around that question - but for now, I have my own. *What if I didn't need to prove myself* - what could I write then, if I had no fear - of being judged, of failing, of falling short?

11

JUST TAKE ONE TINY STEP

e all have those days - you know the ones I mean. When you just tell yourself – "What's the point?" When you feel that everything you're doing is pointless, nothing is working. You want to give up. You want to stop. You feel that you have nothing creative left to give.

I am in the throes of marketing_my latest book and it is not a pleasant experience for me. Sure, there are the moments when someone says they love your book, or you read something and remember why you wrote it in the first place, but most of the time it feels awful. You reach out to people, feeling like you're peddling something unsavory, and question yourself every time you get rejected. Or shut down. Or ignored. Or your emails go unanswered. I know people are busy. I know that no one means it personally. I know all of this intellectually, but it still hurts. It feels personal. I feel rejected.

It's the same sort of feeling when you're looking for a job, and feel like you're sending your CV into the ether, to be sucked up by a black hole that came swimming by just at the right moment. You're writing blog posts, or making music or painting, and you have all this material that no one is reading or listening to or looking at. Or even if they are, they don't respond to it. You create something, and it doesn't resonate. You are desperate for feedback and you hit a stone wall of silence. The world doesn't care - about you or your music or your art or your writing.

We are told that we need to have patience. We need to get really <u>really</u> good before we can expect a lot of traction. Or that it doesn't matter what others think, it only matters that we keep doing the work. Yeah sure, we have heard all that. But it doesn't matter how many times we hear that we need to focus on the process and not the product, that we need to keep creating and eventually we will get better, that fame and fortune are fickle mistresses. We know this, and we still want that flicker of appreciation, that soupçon of encouragement. We need to know that our work matters.

Unfortunately, sometimes we don't always get that. Sometimes we need to keep doing what we are doing, even when the world is oblivious. Sure, we can change strategy, and do something different, and learn a new skill, but at the end of the day, we still need to do something, make something, put something out there.

What do you do when you don't have the heart to take another step? When you want to curl into a ball and go to sleep for a hundred years?

You take one small tiny action.

Can't write a blog post? Write a headline. Can't paint anything? Draw a flower (or a tree or a dog or a squiggle). Can't send another cover letter? Write a recommendation for someone you worked with. Do anything, even the tiniest action. If nothing else, do the laundry. Sweep the floors. Dust out the cobwebs. Even when all you want to do is grab a pint of Rocky Road and zone out to Netflix, postpone your TV viewing for 30 minutes and take one small action, whatever it is.

Chances are once you are done, you will feel just a little

better. You will want to take one more action. Maybe you did the laundry, and now you feel able to start to fold one pile. Maybe you posted a comment on someone's post and it gave you the idea for one of your own, and you can just about gather up the energy to create an outline. Maybe your little doodle of a flower turned into a sketch of an exotic orchid.

We can get easily discouraged. Life can be hard and unfeeling. We may feel isolated, working hard at crafting a life, a creative life, whatever that means for each of us, and we look up to see that there is no one to notice, or commiserate, or acknowledge us.

On those days when the futility of our dreams threaten to overwhelm us, instead of thinking big, we can think small. The tiny action we are contemplating can slip through the dire scenarios we start to imagine. Sure, doodling or drafting won't make much difference to our work, but it doesn't take much effort. We can tell ourselves, I'm just going to take this one little action, and then go back to contemplating how bad everything is. The only thing is – after that first tiny step, things don't seem so bad after all.

In what project can you take a tiny step?

12

WHAT'S THE REAL
GOAL FOR YOUR BOOK?

I have been working on a book that is much harder than I thought it would be. For some reason I thought it would be a quick diversion, something of a palate cleanser between harder and more involved projects. It is not really turning out that way though.

And I think one of the problems I am having is that I don't really know what I am trying to accomplish with the book. Or rather, I forget or get confused while I am actually working on it. I'm in the editing stage at the moment, which is usually the stage that takes me the longest, when I try to corral my rough ideas into shape. In this case, I am struggling because I guess to some extent I didn't really think the book through, and while I am editing I feel like I am constantly fighting something, but I just don't know what.

And then it hit me. I couldn't figure out the goal for the book. I think each book or painting or piece of art you work on has a goal. Or rather you have a goal for it. It could be simple - I want to tell this story. Or it could be a grand ambition - I want to win a prestigious award. Or it could be altruistic - I want to help people lose weight, or get a better job or become happy. You could have multiple goals. Knowing what your goal is makes it easier, because then you have something you are aiming for, something to work towards.

I am struggling because for this book I didn't explicitly name a goal. And therefore I defaulted to my usual goal - which is to have a perfect book. And that never works out well of course, because nothing is perfect. This book is a follow-up to one of my previous books, which I wrote with the goal of just putting down everything I learned about study skills, in the hope that it would help other students. I approached it with a sense of play and fun, and that is most probably why it's my most easy-to-read, accessible, relatable book.

And yet for this book, I complicated it. I was trying to write it quickly. And perfectly. I was trying to do a good job. Instead of trying to simply write a book that hopefully helps those who read it. And that I enjoy writing.

So far, I have to admit, I haven't really enjoyed writing this book. But I think that's mainly a function of my approach, with an impossibly tight deadline and a lot of expectation and stress.

I hope to change all that, now that I have realized this. I am planning to write down my goal for the book, and to use it as my north star while I finish writing it - reminding me that all I want to do is write something that is helpful. The book has already helped me, even though that hadn't been my intention. I do think it can help others too, but first I have to lighten up a bit. Not take myself and it so seriously.

Regardless of what your goal is for a given project or creative endeavor, it will help to clarify it for yourself. In words. Be clear about what you're trying to do, because then it's far more likely that you will achieve that. And you never know, you might be surprised when you clarify what you were trying to do for yourself, that you were actually going in a completely different direction. Fortunately, it is never too late to turn around, to start afresh or simply to tweak your approach.

What are you trying to accomplish with your current piece of writing?

13

———

THE VALUE OF EDITING

I interview authors on my blog and ask them various questions about their writing process. Many of them mention that while they love writing, they hate editing. And after I heard this a few times, I started to wonder why. And what they really meant.

This might sound odd, but I really like the editing process. I feel that it helps me write more reliably.

I find starting on a project - whether the entire work or just a piece of it - intimidating. I imagine how terrible it will be, how I won't get it right and I put off working on it. I even stay away from my computer and my desk, not even opening up the document to work on it.

Now that I have written several books and other large writing projects, I realize that this is a huge obstacle in my mind. I am scared to start. Because I am scared to suck. On the page. I am scared that my work will be so terrible I will be ashamed and never again be able to write anything again. And yet I also want to write my book, very badly. So, here's my problem - how do I work on my project without being deathly afraid to screw up?

I tell myself that I can edit it.

I say to myself that this is just a rough draft. Just some initial notes. I am just adding in a quote or two. Maybe some bullet points. I jot down a paragraph. And another one. But none of this resembles an actual draft in any way. This looks nothing like a piece of finished writing. And periodically as I work, I despair that it ever will.

Always, when I am in the middle of a book or other long project, I start to doubt whether I can reach the end. I ask myself - can I really pull it off? Can I get to the end? I hate my project, I avoid it. I have a lot of coffee and chocolate.

Lately this process has become slightly easier. I have fewer depressing thoughts about the fate of my work. I start to believe that maybe I can get to the other side. That one day quite soon this will look almost like a finished manuscript and be ready to fly out into the world.

And this is all because of the power of editing.

My final drafts have a lot from my first draft in them. The initial ideas, the arguments, the research. Maybe even the structure, with some alterations. But in many ways the final product is unrecognizable when compared to what it had started out as - a group of disjointed, awkward, halting paragraphs stitched together. They often missed transitions. Or the phrasing was misleading. A lot of parts didn't make sense – unless you paid very close attention and filled in some blanks yourself.

While my final draft isn't perfect, and may still have both big-picture flaws and small typos, it is generally quite polished and reads smoothly. Sometimes when I am going over my final draft for a chapter I am taken aback, as I remember how much I struggled with it initially, and how many times I thought that I would never finish it satisfactorily.

To me the process of editing isn't just about fixing spelling errors and punctuation mistakes. When I am editing, once I have the structure and flow of the piece in place, I work hard to polish each sentence. I want to make sure that I haven't left anything out or made a leap in my head that I forgot to write down. Or that I didn't take any knowledge for granted, assuming my reader would know some specialized information that I forgot to include. Or that my phrasing is not awkward, or the tenses mixed up. I take multiple passes over each chapter, sometimes five or six times. I know that seems excessive, but knowing that I can make it better allows me to get through each pass, allows me to acknowledge the obvious flaws and short-comings and focus on fixing the ones I can.

I am working on a book at the moment where I am re-learning this almost every day. I was really struggling with a particular chapter and told myself that it was ok if it turned out to be just mediocre, basically so I could get it done. As I kept working on it, with each iteration it got better and better and now it is of the same quality as the other chapters. To me that seems like a miracle, because only a week or so ago I was thinking I might not get the book done because I couldn't imagine getting the chapter to where it needed to be.

If you see editing as a necessary evil, as the province of oxford commas and prepositions, then you're missing out its true value. To me, editing allows me to take the leap of putting words on the page, even when they don't feel right, even when I am certain my writing is absolute garbage and has no merit whatsoever. The better I get at editing, the more I trust the process, the more I can allow myself to write those crucial first drafts. Like any writer, I get ideas for books all the time. In fact, for years I had many ideas, but never allowed myself to write any of them, because every attempt at putting my thoughts on paper looked amateurish, fell so far short that I believed I couldn't mold it into something viable. Something good. I really regret all the years I spent not writing, for fear that my writing was terrible, that I couldn't get the words to come out just write.

I didn't know about editing then.

I didn't know that I could change the words and polish them. That given enough patience and perseverance, I could turn a terrible draft into a finished product that although not quite as lofty as that in my imagination, was so improved from my initial scratchings as to merit a sense of amazement. I had turned this pile of hay into golden thread.

If you are one of those writers who doesn't like to edit, I suggest that you see editing not as an enemy to do battle with, but an old friend who is there to watch your back, to smoothen the way forward, to give you a boost up. Thank your friend. Buy her a drink. Get to know her better. And let her help you write more regularly and with less drama.

How do you view editing in your writing process?

14
____

DOES BEING PROLIFIC IMPACT QUALITY?

I've read about this idea in a couple of business books: in order to be more successful, it is better to make "little bets", or commit to smaller and more numerous projects, rather than put all your creative eggs in larger, fewer baskets. In entrepreneurial circles this idea is also known as making a *minimum viable product* and putting it out there as quickly as possible.

The obvious extension of this point is also that you are more likely to succeed if you increase the quantity of your creative endeavors. As Smashwords founder Mark Coker puts it, those authors who have more books published by their platform, sell more books. Bloggers know this too, the more posts you have, the more likely you are to increase traffic to your site.

If this is so obvious why doesn't everyone do it? Well, in some ways this is a common strategy, but it's also a common problem - how do I increase my productivity without impacting my quality?

In some ways, certain products like apps can be revised - so you can create an app, and based on user feedback, update and improve it. This can be a better strategy than simply tinkering away in isolation on features that users may not value as much, and wasting time and effort. The same applies to blog posts - if you write a post that didn't quite hit the mark, you can try again tomorrow.

With books, or music records, or movies, the same principle doesn't apply. Once the product is out there, you can't change it, not without considerable expense, and even then, it may be too late. The reviews are already out there. In that case, it makes sense to spend as much time as possible carefully perfecting the product, doesn't it? Don't we always hear of an award-winning author releasing his much anticipated third or fourth book, after a gap of eight or nine years?

The problem then is how to reconcile the two objectives - the need to increase quantity and the desire to maintain quality. Many creative professionals appear to have mastered this dilemma, those who publish a book a year, or one best-selling record after another. According to Wikipedia, James Patterson has written over 200 novels (many of them with co-authors) and sold over 300 million copies of his books. While readers seem to love his books, those in the industry criticize Patterson for his speed of writing, working with collaborators and plot-heavy books. It is quite likely that not all his books are exceptional, but they would need to entertain readers, or they wouldn't buy his books. It's possible however that some are also really terrible. (I can't say for sure not having read any). And perhaps that's the secret to his success, or that of other prolific, creative individuals. You have to be willing to make some really bad art in order to be able to create some truly spectacular stuff. Agatha Christie, one of my favorite authors, wrote 66 detective novels and 14 short story collections. Some of those novels were truly brilliant, but many others were merely a good read, and some quite disappointing (I have read almost all her novels, many of them several times). Perhaps it's not always possible to predict the quality of a book or movie or painting in advance - it is only when it is completed that it's possible to judge it.

As a writer and perfectionist myself, I am not as prolific as I would like to be, mainly because the issue of quality pulls at me. What if what I am working on is truly terrible? Maybe I should let it marinade, and come back to it. I imagine that either prolific artists don't have these sort of thoughts, or as is much more likely, they choose to ignore them, and doggedly complete the project at hand, and immediately start thinking of the next one. Perhaps they have much thicker skin, and are not as affected by negative criticism. Perhaps they know that they may not be able to control the outcome of their work, but they can certainly control their own effort, and hope that it is enough.

This year, I am resolved to aim for a little less perfection, a little more pragmatism, and hope that I learn habits that let me look back in the years to come at my own substantial body of work.

15

HOW TO KNOW IF YOU
ARE IN A CREATIVE RUT

As creative professionals, we assume that our biggest problem, will probably be that we are taking too many risks. The risk of not having financial security. The risk of doing work that makes people uncomfortable. The risk of not investing enough in marketing ourselves and our work. You may even think that being in a rut by being too *risk averse* could never happen to you.

The funny thing about human beings is that we are incredible at adapting to our environment. We start off in a new situation, we are nervous, maybe scared, then we figure things out. Slowly the new situation becomes comfortable, we get the hang of it, and before we know it, we are in a rut.

Doing research for my most book on study skills, I learned how this really works in our brain. When we are doing something new, learning a new skill, adapting to a new environment, our brains need a way to create a shortcut, a way to remember and execute the actions we need to easily. So each time we do something new, maybe play a certain tune on the piano, or give a speech, we strengthen the white matter or myelin in our brains for that action (see the excellent book *The Talent Code* for a thorough explanation of this phenomenon). The more times we repeat a certain action, the more we strengthen myelin and the easier it gets to play that particular tune or give that particular speech.

So let's say the first few months or year of creating custom social media banners for clients, or designing infographics, you are challenging yourself, coming up with new ideas, really pushing the boundaries of your own skill set. Then, you start to get into a groove. Your work is appreciated, the checks keep coming in, and you are confident about your abilities. At this point you are feeling good. The work is piling up, you don't have time to look around, to see what is missing, what you are not doing.

But the problem is, that you might be in a rut, and you don't even realize it.

I was reading Shonda Rhimes' excellent memoir *The Year of Yes*, and in the book, she talks about how although her creative career was going brilliantly, in every other aspect of her life, she was stuck in a rut. She was afraid of trying new things, of saying yes to new opportunities, from the fear of messing it up or being vulnerable. I recognized myself in that description - I had become afraid to try anything new, to venture outside my comfort zone. The only difference is, that I was doing this in my creative life.

I have written six books so far, and all of them have been very different from each other. I haven't just been doing the same thing over and over. So why do I think I haven't taken the risks? Because I was afraid to write something that revealed more of myself, that would require me to be more vulnerable. I wrote from my head, but not my heart. To the extent that I have revealed myself and my deeply held beliefs in my writing, it has been better received than my other work. But I still haven't really been able to take a risk and really share more of the real me.

Not everyone gets creatively stuck in the same ways. For some people it could be that without realizing it, they have stopped trying to venture into different aspects of their field, and just keep doing the work that is safe and pays the bills. For others, it might mean that they are stuck reading the same books, meeting the same people, watching the same TV shows, and are not cultivating any new experiences. For some, it could even be something as simple as being unexcited about their work, being bored and wishing for something external to excite them again.

If you feel like you're falling out of love with your work, or your life, sometimes all you need is a simple shift in perspective. In Rhimes' memoir, she explains that her shift came when she realized that she simply needed to start saying yes to things, even or especially when, they scared her. For me, recently, a shift in perspective happened when I decided to simply try things that I was interested in, without demanding that I do them brilliantly or that they were immediately successful.

One of the results of this decision was that I finally started to do interviews of authors on my blog, something that I was really interested in doing, but avoided earlier for fear of adding to my workload and taking away from my book writing. Yes, it is a lot of work. But reaching out to so many different authors, I am learning a lot, and the whole process has been a blast.

So if you are doing creative work of some kind, and feel like you have got into a rut, try to do something that you have always wanted to and haven't either had the courage to do or made the time. Start a side project that has no commercial value. Do something that is just for you. Alternatively, mix up your creative inputs. Join a group where you are likely to meet totally different people. Read books in a genre you never considered before - maybe read non-fiction if you only read fiction or the other way around. Ask friends for recommendations for good podcasts or shows that wouldn't usually come up on your radar. Take an online course.

All of this is time-consuming and disruptive to your normal routine. And that is kind of the point. We are busy, more than ever, and there is a never-ending list of things to get done. But at the end of the day, what each of us really wants, is to do something inspiring, to leave a legacy, to touch someone, even just one person. In order to do this, we need to expand ourselves, get out of our own head and do something unexpected. We need to have what Zen Buddhists call "beginner's mind", where you look at something from a fresh perspective, when you are open to learning and to the possibility of life.

What do you do when you feel stuck creatively?

16

———

MUCH ADO ABOUT WRITER'S BLOCK

uch has been written about writer's block. In fact, I have spent countless hours seeking out books and searching online for ideas that will help me to beat it. Over time, I have realized that writer's block is really another name for perfectionism. You can't put anything down on paper, or type anything on the screen, because everything you can think of to say sounds wrong even before you've written it. The longer you sit in front of the blank page or screen in front of you, the harder it gets to put something down, and eventually, you just get up in frustration, telling yourself that you are blocked.

Incidentally, I am a master at writer's block. I spent years planning the first chapter, the first scene of a memoir that I wanted to write. This was going to be my first book, my most important book. If I didn't nail the first scene, then the book wouldn't come together. I never thought of writing the chapters I did know how to write, and simply putting the initial chapter in place later. Eventually, of course, I did employ that approach, and wrote other books; but because of that thinking I lost years of writing time.

Perfectionism in writing is an insidious thing. It creeps up in the guise of "standards". Who wouldn't want to write well? Or ensure that they do a good job?

But there is a difference between having standards and perfectionism. Having standards implies that you care about quality, maybe you go over your work one more time, you take extra care while editing, you strive harder to get better as a writer. Perfectionism tells you that you have to get it right in one draft. There is no room for improvement, no room for error. With that attitude, no wonder we freeze up when faced with the prospect of having to write a first sentence. We stare at the blank page, aware of the importance of that first sentence and think – "This has to grab the reader. This has to be witty and entertaining and shed light into the mysteries of life". No wonder we are paralyzed.

How do you get away from perfectionism? You remind yourself that what you're working on is just a draft. I had a law professor who introduced our class to the concept of the *zero draft*. This was the stage even before the first draft, where you just put some thoughts down, noodle with ideas and directions in which to angle the essay.

Even though the term first draft has the word "draft" in it, most people including myself, associate it with the final or near-final version of something. The same connotation weirdly doesn't apply to zero drafts. Starting with a zero draft gives you permission to write an unpolished, messy draft. Ever since I first learned about the concept, I always started my academic papers, and later my books, with a zero draft.

Which hasn't stopped me from needing several other drafts as well. When asked how many drafts a piece of writing might need, writing coach Hilary Rettig said, "As many as it takes".

I think the best way to combat the tendency towards perfectionism in your writing is to give yourself permission - permission to write something that needs to be edited. Permission to write something that isn't quite finished yet. And permission to write and publish something that isn't perfect, but is something better - it represents you.

How do you deal with writer's block?

17

WHEN TO JUDGE YOUR WORK

When you're doing creative work, whether it is writing a novel or creating a beautiful piece of pottery, it's easy to fall into the trap of judging your work and yourself too harshly. After all, we decide to work in an area that we ourselves love - you long to create beautiful art inspired by the work of others, or write stories that make you feel the way your favorite novel or movie does. You know what is good, and when you fail to see it in your own work it can be heart-breaking. You criticize your work, holding it up to the high standards you know you like in the work of others and aspire to see in your own work.

However, judging your work while working on it can be brutal to the creative process. You try to make whimsical connections and let your imagination run free, while the critic on your shoulder sternly commands that you get back to the straight and narrow path, don't run after stupid ideas that haven't been tried before and might possibly lead you to fail epically. This critic always fails to mention that your whimsical ideas might lead you to do something so different that it takes people's breath away, that you could succeed beyond your wildest dreams. That by stamping out the possibility of jumping off a cliff, it is also stamping out the possibility of your work taking off soaring over the edge.

On the other hand, you don't want to be so in love with your work that you can't see any flaws, stopping you from growing and improving at your craft.

Blogger and lifelong learner Scott Young wrote an article on this topic that I thought proposed a good balance between maintaining humility and having the will to keep working. His theory is that we should judge our past work with the same sense of critique that we might bring to someone else's work - taking note of missteps to correct in the future. When we are composing our current work however, we should avoid critiquing it harshly, especially as that might prevent us from having the will to complete it.

As a writer I can see the flaw in this - that if I don't critique my work while I'm doing it, won't I end up putting out work that isn't good enough, thereby affecting my own reputation? On the other hand, with each project I go through phases where I'm convinced that the work is terrible and there's no point in continuing. Usually a looming deadline and the specter of angry colleagues forces me to push through these feelings and complete the project - and the end product is much better than I thought it would be.

When I don't have an external deadline, and the only person who will be disappointed if I don't finish is me, it's harder to silence the voice that whispers in my ear that the work is really terrible and that I should abandon it pronto. Often, if I can ignore it, I will end up with work that really is quite good, even though I can always further improve it. I won't get that chance though, if I get demotivated enough by my self-criticism to give up before I can finish. At any rate, every project that I have completed, even the ones on which I can look back and cringe that I had the temerity to write such drivel, have taught me so much about writing.

Thus, whatever reservations I may have about sacking my inner Judge Judy for the duration of my project, is tempered by the thought that it will be that much easier to get to the finish line. Besides, there is probably a lot of truth to the saying that you can catch more flies with a drop of honey than a gallon of gall. Shouldn't the same advice apply to nurturing our creative instincts? After all, a little honey may go a long way towards getting me closer to finishing my work-in-progress.

18

TAKE STEPS, NOT LEAPS

We often think of being creative or innovative as taking a giant leap forward from the status quo - be that our own or others. We write a best-selling book, or create a product that wows everyone, or discover a cure for a deadly disease. One moment there was the old, and the next there is this new, improved, radically different 'thing' that we have created. We believe, therefore, that we need to become capable of these huge leaps -and we think, how can _I_ write a best-selling book, or design an incredible product? The pressure mounts, and we reject plenty of good ideas right off the bat, because none of them sound like the next big thing. *Not yet anyway.*

What I learned, from this book I am reading by Kevin Ashton: *How To Fly A Horse: The Secret History of Creation, Invention and Discovery,* and serendipitously, from a few other sources as well, that big changes happen in small steps. You take one step forward in a direction that seems promising, then you re-evaluate, learn something new, make some changes and take another step forward. This may not seem glamorous, may not make for good storytelling, but it is closer to the truth than the proverbial light-bulb moment.

Well you may be saying, most of us have had a light-bulb moment or two. So what about that then? Those don't count do they? Well, actually they do - but they usually don't account for creating the entire work. Maybe you start with a spark of an idea for something, but the rest has to be worked out by you, painstakingly, one page or note or prototype at a time. And that initial idea - it probably wasn't a giant leap. Most of my ideas are just one step up from a book I read, or an amalgamation of several books and articles and things bouncing around in my head. Nothing just comes completely out of the blue that is 30 steps away from what I'm doing. And here's the thing - when it does – I'm just not ready for it.

I had an idea for a book on philosophy in college, while I was studying legal theory. The idea was so big, to me at least, that it scared me. I didn't think I knew enough, or had enough ability, to write this book. This book stayed with me over the years, I was really excited about it and I kept telling myself that I should start working on it, but really I never did. It was still too big for me. Now I don't really feel that it is too big anymore, but I have lost most of my excitement about the book. The ideas no longer feel like such a leap - there are similar ideas out there now, even if in different forms.

Maybe I should have pursued that idea more. But maybe there is also a lesson here - that when things are genuinely a leap, we may be intimidated into not following up. Or there is a lot of pressure – I'm going to be the next Stephen King, not I'm going to write a fun, kooky story and see where it goes. Or you don't yet have the tools to take the leap - like I felt handicapped by my lack of background in philosophy - but you might have the courage to take a small step - maybe I could have written the introduction, or the easiest chapter. Or even turned it into a blog post. Many books that I love started out as blog posts that resonated enough with readers that they then evolved into a book.

So go on, take a step in the direction you want to go, and don't worry that your shoes are itty-bitty and delicate and your step is only small and tentative. You are moving forward, and if you keep stepping, maybe you'll get there faster than any leap.

19

NEEDING A TRIBE

There is a lot of talk on blogs and in business books about finding your "tribe" - a group of people with whom you can identify and who form the natural audience for your work. There is a lot of merit to this idea; however, it is usually discussed in the context of networking in the business world.

It is equally important to find your tribe as a creative professional no matter what stage you are at. At an event that I attended recently (the launch of a book in which I have a co-authored chapter), I met an ex-colleague who is now also a full-time fiction writer. We hadn't met in a long time, and amidst catching up on life events we discussed some of the vagaries of the writing process, and the life of being a writer. It was a short dialogue, as the primary purpose of the event was to network, and I had to leave shortly after.

The few minutes I spent casually discussing perspectives with another writer, even though she writes in very different genres, was more validating than I had imagined. I don't belong to a writer's group, for various reasons primarily related to worrying that I will psych myself out of writing in some way. I find it hard enough to write without undue pressure and questions regarding my work.

In fact, that was partly what we talked about. My friend, the fiction writer, writes what I would classify as literary fiction, while I write primarily non-fiction. I always imagined that the approach and the experiences would be different writing such different material - but when I heard her describing her challenges with her current book, I could instantly relate. More so, it validated many of my own concerns.

I am confident that the need for acknowledgement, the need to share daily struggles exists in every creative endeavor. While some are more naturally collaborative mediums, some arts require weeks and months of solitary effort to produce something. Often the end product may be less than what you imagined, or it may not be received as well as you were hoping. At such times, the journey has to be worth it, because for now it may be all you have. It really helps to hear that from someone other than your family, which is where the tribe comes in. A timely reassurance, the acknowledgement that someone else is going through the same thing, may keep you going for a little while longer, hopefully long enough to finally create that masterpiece!

Who is in your tribe and when do you reach out to them?

20

OBSTACLES TO CREATIVITY

*A*rtists, and indeed anyone trying something new, taking some risks, going out on a limb, face obstacles as a matter of course. The only problem is that every time we face them, we are surprised, unprepared and more than a little annoyed at the disruption to our routine and plan.

Obstacles can be in the form of an unexpected event taking precious time away from a deadline, like the family emergency that happened to me at the beginning of the month, taking away two weeks of time from my deadline, and even more time trying to regain my previous momentum. They can be in the form of a sudden illness, or a last minute request from a client or boss, that may threaten to derail your present assignment. While I am finalizing this book, the world is in the middle of a once-in-a-generation global pandemic, which no doubt derailed the creative efforts of many people, me included.

Obstacles may also come up in your creative arsenal – your laptop starts to give trouble, freezes or becomes agonizingly slow just as the last hours of the deadline creep up on you; you discover that you're out of the exact shade of fabric you needed for a crucial detail; or, as I have been facing recently, you get carpal tunnel and find it difficult to type or hold a pen.

Our tools are everything to us, and when they don't work or we forget a crucial implement in our toolkit, it can be beyond frustrating. It can be debilitating. The first thought at such a time is to curse, get angry and blame sundry forces that are conspiring against you.

However, I have come to believe that obstacles are actually there to help you even though it's tough to see this initially. They are there to test your resolve, to see if you really have what it takes to complete your project. It's not supposed to be a test that you fail, if you recognize it for what it is; a way to check in with yourself if you have the conviction to follow through and go all the way. If you do, the obstacles become a challenge, something you are anxious to overcome, to triumph over and send packing.

When the project is over, when you have crossed the finish line, the obstacles that you have overcome are what you will look back on with pride, and they will fuel your sense of accomplishment. So look at them with appreciation, and tell yourself that whatever you're facing is actually a sign that you're getting close to the end of the road.

21

———————

WRITING THROUGH IT ALL

I am working on a book project right now that is really close to me, and something I have been working on on and off for years, even decades. Perhaps because it is so important to me, I have been having a miserable time of it lately. I have been working on it so long, I just want it to be done. I have other projects and plans in the pipeline, things I have moved to make room for this. I also feel that I have a lot of credibility riding on this. All these are *not* ingredients for fast flowing writing.

I'm working on my nth draft of the book, and although it does keep getting better, each time I begin to feel more discouraged. Things were going swimmingly a few days ago, but suddenly every minute I spend on this feels like a few hours. I am typing up some notes I wrote by hand into Scrivener, and I am hating it - mainly because the book feels terrible to me. It's almost like I'm wading through a thick river of mud, with weighted boots, and each step is getting harder and harder. When working on it, I end up feeling guilty because I know that I really need to make faster progress.

Last night, I started writing down some notes for another

project I have been toying with, thinking the distraction would do me good, maybe make it easier to get back to this book. I went to bed feeling pleased with the progress I made, as I fleshed out the structure for that book. I had told myself that I'm not writing it now, but I also know that if I don't write down my ideas now and make some progress while I can, the book probably won't ever get written. And if I'm not going to ever write it, what's the harm in noodling around with it anyway, just for a bit? That let me go for it, and I felt like the words were flowing.

Back to my main project today, and it's still not coming together. Today the pump feels stuck, like the pipe is clogged and the words are falling out in a clump, thick and sluggish.

I guess I simply have to trust in my writing. Do what Sage Cohen said in one of her books – "Let someone else decide whether it's any good. Let me just do the work." If this is truly the best I can do, then procrastinating is pointless. Waiting to be inspired is pointless. There is only one thing to do - write through it. Some days are good, and the words flow like music, and other days, you wonder why you chose this vocation (even though it really feels like it chose you).

This is what Steven Pressfield means by going pro. You put the words down even when everything is falling apart in your personal life, and you are lying in bed with cramps and a hot water bottle, and when you are convinced that what you're writing is the worst drivel ever to be produced. You write through all that, and then you deserve to call yourself a writer.

So for today, I am a writer, although I really don't know how I will feel tomorrow. Or five minutes from now. But for now, I am writing.

22

BALANCING THE WELL

*J*ulia Cameron wrote in one of her books about "filling the well", filling ourselves on art and images and creative input, so that we are brimming with fresh ideas and creativity for our own projects. This is the premise behind her concept of *Artist's Dates* - spending time on your own doing something creative like visiting a gallery or a bookstore or watching a play.

Although I never liked to go on formal artist dates, I have noticed that if I go too long without fresh creative input, I start to feel stale and dispirited. It starts to infect my work, even if I am working on something dry like a journal article. Taking the time to fill my well, even if it's as simple as watching a movie that is quite different from the kind I usually watch, can inject fresh enthusiasm and ideas.

I have even started to intuitively feel the level at which my well is filled - half, three-quarters, full to the brim. When I am feeling full to the brim with ideas and thoughts, I can actually overcome the usual crippling writer's block that assails me most of the time. Skipping with enthusiasm and admiration for the talent and creativity of others' work, I feel slightly braver and want to attempt my own. To me, this is the main advantage of filling the well - keeping the sniping Critic at bay.

The flip side of this however, is that you can be endlessly filling the well, but never drawing from it. It's much less risky to keep reading books, watching movies and listening to other people's music, and never putting yourself on the line by attempting any art of your own. You end up overflowing your well - you keep adding to it, but never withdrawing and using any of the creative sparks generated by all this input. Without output of a fairly regular nature, you aren't able to use the excess input, which simply drains away.

This was me for many years, and am even now guilty of it sometimes. It can be tempting to have lots of exciting ideas, write them down on a notepad or Evernote, and then keep diving into ever more exciting creative entrées, gorging on the smorgasbord of art available for consumption in the digital age. You may think by writing the idea down you have made sure it doesn't escape, but what about the raw material of injected creativity which is now lost? It's like a dancer warming up for a dance session, and then sitting on the sofa and watching a documentary on the History Channel. The effort put into the warm-up is wasted if the dancer doesn't then practice her dance routine, taking advantage of her warmed up muscles.

Creating art needs a delicate balance - we must take in enough input to keep the ideas flowing, keeping our muscles warm and ready, and we must also exercise those muscles on a regular basis to be ready for the fabulous ideas when they come to us - fed on a mulch of great art. The past few weeks I had been dangerously close to overfilling the well, but a spate of deadline-driven productivity in the past week has withdrawn enough to keep the well just at three-quarters level. I believe that has earned me a curl-up in my bed with a good book - just as soon as I outline my next book chapter.

Where are you on the spectrum - filling your well too little or too much?

23

____

PAYING THE PRICE TO SUCCEED

*A*fter I got the highest grades in India's equivalent of the O-level exams (in 10th grade), and received a bunch of prizes in high school, for years classmates and casual acquaintances would remark: "Oh, how lucky you are to be so smart. I could never get such good grades!" The first few times I heard this I cringed, thinking, *if only you knew that it wasn't like that.* After the first dozen times, I began to feel peeved. Sure, I wouldn't always express my irritation; instead, I would smile tightly and say "Thanks". But what I really wanted to say was this: "It's not a question of being smart. I worked my tail off for those grades, after starting near the bottom of the class. You could have done it too if you had worked that hard."

I was reminded recently of this feeling while reading best-selling author of motivational books Brian Tracy's book *No Excuses: The Power of Self-Discipline*. It is an inspiring book, and I would highly recommend it, if you can handle the tough love approach. Anyway, having said that, in the book the author talks about "paying the price for success". He says that if you want to be successful in a certain area, just figure out what the price for success is, and then pay it.

I realize this sounds overly simplistic, and can even offend some people, but when I read this advice, I was jolted out of my complacency. I love to complain about things and explain, to myself and others, why I can't change something or make something happen. I feel stressed about the quality of my writing, or how many books I sell, among other things. And while in general I believe that we can change aspects of our lives, when it comes to specific areas I'd like improvements in, I love to trot out the excuses, and list everything I have already tried to change the situation, which haven't worked. Reading this particular sentence, I realized however, that it wasn't about what I had or hadn't done already. The question I needed to ask myself was simple – *Did I know what the price for success was in this instance, and was I willing to pay it?*

Let me illustrate. Let's say you need or want to lose a significant amount of weight. While weight loss is an emotional minefield for most people, and there are many legitimate and not-so-legitimate reasons why people find it difficult (trust me, I *totally* get it), if you are honest with yourself, you know what the price for weight loss is, at least in most instances. It means making time in a busy schedule to exercise (even when that's the last thing you feel like or have the energy for). It means giving up dessert most of the occasions when you want to indulge, especially when everything in your life is falling apart and a slice of cake is everything you're looking forward to. It means learning to like to eat vegetables, and substituting fruit and yogurt (or insert healthy option here) for your favorite high-calorie snack. It means a lot of little sacrifices and tough choices that aren't so little and seem overwhelming to someone who has tried and failed many times before. But the question isn't whether it is easy or doable – the question is whether paying that price will get you closer to your goal. And if you're honest, you know it will. Now, depending on your current circumstances, you may not be able to or want to pay that price, but even framing it in those terms makes the actions you take seem like choices, not simply a hand that has been dealt to you.

As I thought about all this, and pondered all the areas in my life that are stuck, or that I am frustrated about, I started to remember times when I did succeed. And every single one that I can currently bring to mind, I did pay the price for that success. Whether it was spending hours in the library and declining invites to the pub to get through my difficult courses in grad school, or chaining myself to my desk and staying up till the wee morning hours to complete a book or waking up at 4am to get ready and travel for two hours by bus to rehearse for a cultural show that brought me friends and lifelong memories of an exhilarating and memorable performance. None of these accomplishments were easy, and while I was going through them, there were countless moments when I wanted to give up. But luckily I didn't. I paid the price. And got so much out of it.

And that brings me to the most important realization. I often don't remember the price I paid. I intellectually remember how difficult it was. But the emotional pain is no longer there. I remember the thought that it was really tough, but I don't remember the feeling of hardship. I do remember, and still benefit from, the outcome – the memories, the experience, the boost to my resume. The price I paid doesn't seem such a high price now, though that wasn't the case at the time I was paying it. Some days it seemed like no matter how hard I worked, I wasn't making any progress. Some days I didn't think I would make it another day. I thought about quitting, and if I wasn't going to be letting down a lot of people, I probably would have. But I kept going, and in the end, it seemed worth it.

In terms of having the creative life I want, perhaps I need to ask the same question. What is the price I need to pay – whether my goal is to write and publish more books or to become a bestselling author – and am I willing to pay that price? Granted some goals aren't entirely in my control. For instance, I couldn't decide to win awards and then work towards achieving them. But I could decide to improve my craft, whether that meant taking writing courses or via some other method.

Quite often we look at the success of someone else and feel envious of what they have achieved. However, if we truly are honest with ourselves, we know what they have had to sacrifice to get there, and equally that we aren't willing to do the same.

Perhaps then having the passion to really succeed at something really means that you are willing to learn what the price to succeed at something is, and pay it. Many athletes, for instance, watch their diets really carefully and spend their days on rigid training schedules. For artists, the price we pay might be sacrificing all our free time to our art, or learning to overcome our fears and interacting with peers and potential readers on social media.

It doesn't matter what you choose to do, just remember that we all have more choices than we think we do, and though we may not be able to control everything, we can control more than we realize.

24

REGAINING MOMENTUM
ON A CREATIVE PROJECT

I'm getting quite close to the wire on a long-term creative project that has already had several delays, and for which I set a deadline of November for it to be completed in its entirety. In August, I was finally starting to make good progress, and the last few days of the month my fingers were flying on the keyboard as I started to pile up the word counts.

And then I had a family emergency and had to travel to India. (Note: this chapter was originally written much before the pandemic and consequent travel restrictions.) It was a stressful time, and there was a lot to be done, and work on my project halted completely. I was fine to put aside the project temporarily, promising myself that I would pick it up again when I got back home. And yet it's been more than ten days since I have been back, and attempting to pick up the thread on my project. I've completely lost my momentum.

I can't for the life of me get back to the pace I was working at before I left, and I can't even summon up the same level of motivation I had on the project as before. I know intellectually that I still need to meet the deadline, and need to work even harder than before to make up the time shortfall. And yet, I'm dragging my feet as it were, and languidly typing a few sentences at a time.

Usually, I read books on writing when this happens, but the standard advice on working a little every day isn't helping, because I am behind schedule and need to figure out a way to get a *lot* done every day. Writing teacher Julia Cameron has said that "writing rights things", and in this instance, not writing is making me grumpy and I'm finding fault with every aspect of my life. It's quite likely that these faults were already there, but when I was writing, they weren't so visible to me.

I tried taking a break – I took a day off to read a book, just relax and not fixate on my deadline. The next day I got more done, but the lack of energy and lethargy came back the day after that. I don't really have any other tricks up my sleeve – other than the old favorite – powering through. I will keep sitting down at my computer, until the pace picks up and I start to fall in love with the material again. I've read enough interviews of writers to know that this happens to many people, and they get through it, and I will too. It's just that now I know this intellectually, but in my heart I still have this gnawing feeling: "What if I can't finish this book on time? Should I just give up now?" These feelings are scary – and my instinct is to tamp down on them and ignore them. But I know from experience, not acknowledging feelings just encourages them to grow, so here I am doing the opposite – and strangely I feel a bit better already. It's like when the sun comes up, the monsters that freaked you out the night before feel like silly shadows that disappear in the light of the sun's rays.

25

WHEN THE WORK STOPS BEING FUN

I have been working on a book that I started as a labor of love, and yet lately it has become an object of despair. I am dragging my feet, unable to make progress, and yet I am stubborn, so I can't make myself stop working on it, or put it aside and do something else. For some reason, I get panicky at the idea of just leaving it and taking a break, maybe watching a movie, or going for a long walk. I have this idea that by leaving the general vicinity of my desk, I am risking letting go of the moment when suddenly I will want to write, when the words will simply flow. I am like a restless animal, pacing around my territory, but unable to settle down.

The book has taken over all my thoughts while I am awake, leaving room for nothing else. I have stopped having ideas, stopped being frivolous and fun, and even just having conversations with people is really draining. In short, the work is no longer fun, and neither am I.

In desperation, I picked up an old favorite, Julia Cameron's *The Right to Write*. In it she describes hitting "The Wall". The Wall is a block that comes up when we become acutely aware of the book and start to over-identify with it. As I neared the end of the book, I started going slower and slower, because I secretly got scared. I started evaluating every section and sentence based on its reception – a terrible way to write if there was one. And by cutting myself off from anything else that I enjoyed, I was making it harder for my heart to engage with the work – I just "wanted to be done". In fact, that's what I kept telling anyone who asked.

Julia's solution (yes, I think of her as a wonderful, warm friend I can simply call up on the telephone to receive her spot-on advice): become humble. Get over The Wall by going under it – leave your ego behind. Be willing to write badly.

The way I interpret it is this: Be willing to take a risk, and stand out. Be willing to not be perfect. Be willing to be human.

This attitude is hard to remember or sustain – I keep falling back under the spell of "what if it's not perfect?" I don't want to deliberately write badly, but writing is subjective. Sure, I can ensure that the footnotes are correct and I have spelled every word correctly. But other than that – there are a million deci-sions that I have made in the course of writing, which if I tried to second-guess, I would be stuck forever. Is there a perfect choice for every decision – how to start the introduction, what word to use in the sub-heading? Perhaps I am overthinking all of this, but I believe that overthinking is what most writers do best. Even though these thoughts keep swirling around my head, I try to remember that the goal is to do the best job I can right now, but the goal is also *to finish*. An unfinished book doesn't help anyone.

So how do I capture the fun in my work again? Focus on the interesting little sections – usually also the bits where I have to take a risk. Look at this interesting observation I made – where do I include it? What about these recommendations – how should I phrase them? Instead of thinking of them as mistakes waiting to happen, I could think of them as the reward – the quirky bits of my book that make it unique, which is why I started writing it in the first place.

And it doesn't hurt to find some external sources of fun either. In my case – I bought a box of cheap oil pastels and some paper to experiment with. I'm really not very good at art, but I love playing around with different materials and seeing what I can create. The fun I am having just doing something new is slowly seeping into my work as well.

So what do you do when the work stops being fun?

[move this further below]

26

POSITIVE PSYCHOLOGY
FOR WRITERS

I have been reading a few books on principles that derive from positive psychology, or as some call it "the science of happiness", hoping to find ways to apply what I learned to writing.

As I understand it, positive psychology focuses on positive emotions and how to increase them. Now I am going to make the assumption that if you are a writer, you choose to do it because it makes you happy. Unlike many other professions, writing isn't full of obvious perks like a company car and the corner office, so usually people choose to be writers for intrinsic reasons. So then, writing is supposed to make you happy. If it already does, that's great, and you can skip further to my next point. If it doesn't, then a good question to ask yourself is why.

But first, does it matter if you are happy while writing? Our culture is filled with examples that connect writers to negative vices - the alcoholic writer, the solitary writer who refuses to engage with people, the starving artist who can't make ends meet. None of these connotations are positive, and sometimes we believe that's the only way to be a serious, professional writer. Then there are the quotes on writing – "You just need to stare at a blank piece of paper till drops of blood start to form on your forehead". Not exactly encouraging a positive outlook.

Positive psychology states that optimism and a positive mindset are more conducive to creativity than pessimism and being negative. You have more ideas and you are more original when you are feeling positive.

The other useful lesson I learned from positive psychology is that we are happier and more productive when we focus on our strengths. This might be obvious, but I often find that I obsess a lot more about my weaknesses than hone in on my strengths. I keep thinking of all the things I can't do, what I am not good at. I can't do social media, I am not great at marketing, I can't write popular fiction like XYZ author. I focus on my low sales figures, all the aspects of marketing I am not doing, all the platforms I am not on. I read a wonderful book and then fret because I could never write in that genre.

However, positive psychology states that focusing on your strengths can make you feel better about yourself and you end up succeeding more. So instead, I should be focusing on the aspects of writing that I enjoy and am good at, without looking at other authors. Write the book that I want to read. Successful indie author Joanna Penn has said that she always thought that writing literary fiction was what she was supposed to do, even though what she loved to read were thrillers. She ignored her initial instincts, and today she is a USA Today bestselling author of Dan Brown-esque thrillers.

To me, focusing on your strengths means being honest with yourself about what you are good at, what you can become better at, and what you are better off outsourcing or just forgetting about. Write the books you really want to. Hone your craft and get better at your writing, but only in the areas you really care about or are interested in. And outsource anything that you absolutely hate doing so that you can spend more time on the aspects of writing you love and get better at that. If Facebook really isn't your thing, don't force yourself to be on it. Spend time on writing a lovely author newsletter and send that out every month instead. If you can't get the hang of converting your books to print, outsource that and start writing your next novel.

Another aspect of positive psychology is gratitude. This is something that I personally struggle with a lot - I find it hard to be grateful, especially when I am focusing on all the lack in my life. Like the poor sales of my books, or how slowly I am making progress on my current book, or how I wish I was doing better on social media and improving my author platform. However, changing how you think can change not only your mood but also your environment. There is so much to be grateful for if only we take the time to see it. We have the opportunity to write a book and put it out within 24 hours, and have readers from around the world read our books. We can sell our books in different formats, and even translate them into other languages. Instead of honing in on poor sales or slow promotion campaigns, we can choose to be grateful for every reader that buys our books, and every follower on social media. We can celebrate every fan email or positive mention of our work online. We can be thankful for every reader who took the time to post a review. It can be hard to stand out as an author and get our work noticed, but we are lucky to have so many opportunities that were unavailable even ten years ago. Let's savor every good thing instead of only complaining or worrying about the bad.

I am also learning from positive psychology to be less critical of my work. To be able to see the good parts, or at the very least, to reserve judgement while I am still in the draft stages. To edit with a light touch. To be optimistic about the merit of my work, instead of giving in to the voice that says that my work is terrible, that no one will read it, that writing the book is a waste of my time. I am trying to remind myself that this is only a draft, I can always do it over. I try to remember all the good things people have said about my work, instead of fixating on the negatives. None of this is easy, but all of it is worth it.

Whether you call it the law of attraction, positive psychology, optimism or being a dreamer, anything that makes it easier and more pleasurable to write, is worth trying, in my opinion. Focus on the positive aspects of your writing, give more time to your strengths, be grateful and try to cultivate a more positive mindset. Your writing and your author career can only improve as a result.

27

LESSONS FROM
AUSTEN ON WRITING

Recently I picked up Jane Austen's *Northanger Abbey* to re-read it – I think I read it in high school although I really have no recollection of the story. I am ashamed to say this time around I gave up a chapter into it – I found it difficult to read, despite knowing that it was an Austen novel. Now before any rabid Austen fans start sending me threats by email, I want to clarify – I am a huge, huge fan of her work – well some of her work. *Pride and Prejudice* is undoubtedly one of the best novels ever written, and as far as I am concerned, perfect, because not a single sentence is out of place or superfluous.

I've read about how we should not judge the works of famous creators simply on the basis of their most famous work, but also take into account their lesser known and perhaps not as polished work. It's difficult to think of this in abstract terms, especially as we tend to have a static view of talent – we are always saying of this or the other person, "She is so talented!" or "He is a brilliant writer!" As if that were a steady state phenomenon – you were born brilliant and remained so your whole life. The corollary to this sentiment being, of course, that if you haven't achieved anything of brilliance yet, you are highly unlikely to do so in the future.

I intellectually know that this is not true, but sometimes working on my own projects it feels true. I feel as if no matter how much I try, I can never reach those dizzy heights to which I aspire. After all, how could I begin to compete against JK Rowling or Suzanne Collins or Sara Gruen?

Reading or trying to read *Northanger Abbey* gave me a lot of hope – it is a novel that has none of the breezy, easy style of *Pride and Prejudice*, and yet Austen wrote it after her first draft of *Pride and Prejudice* (initially titled <u>*First Impressions*</u>). She shows that it is possible to be a great writer without everything you write automatically being great. If you've read biographies of Austen, you know that she revised her books several times and kept working on them for years. Her early work differs from her later more polished prose significantly. If a writer such as Austen struggled with her prose, and needed endless revisions, then there is hope for the rest of us.

THE SECOND LESSON I learnt from Austen comes from a book by Lori Smith titled *The Jane Austen Guide to Life*. In the book, the author describes just how difficult it was for Austen to get published, and how disconcerting it must have been for her. Anyone who has ever received a rejection of any sort knows how it feels. It is almost impossible to get up the courage to try again, knowing the outcome might turn out to be the same.

Austen lived at a time when women were not only not expected to work, they were actively discouraged from it. And writing (and reading) novels was definitely frowned upon. It would have been only too easy for her to decide to simply not try to publish her work, and just enjoy the adulation of her family without risking the pain of rejection.

Isn't this something we can easily relate to? How often have we decided against doing something for ourselves that isn't easy, something that will cause friction and upset the equilibrium. We ask ourselves – do I really need to go back to school? Should I take an evening art class when I could be spending more time with my family? Can I really make diet food just for myself and not eat with my family? It's easy to give in to the status quo, to not want to make waves in our lives, at home and at the workplace. But in our hearts we know that we want to get another degree, to go back to our love for art, to lose weight and feel good about ourselves. Why then do we not take the risk?

This is the lesson that Austen taught us – and I am grateful that she did – because I cannot imagine a world in which Austen's novels, _all_ her novels, don't exist. She gave us this gift, and so must you – give the world the gift of whatever it is you are afraid to pursue with all your heart and resources – for we don't know what art (in the full sense of the word) we could be missing out on.

28

DON'T LEARN FROM OTHERS IN YOUR FIELD

This is going to sound like very strange advice, and goes against conventional wisdom, but I'm going to say it anyway: you should not try to learn from others in your field. In fact, you should go out of your way to avoid them altogether.

Ok, I will clarify my extraordinary statement: you should not learn from others in your field *in certain circumstances*. What are they?

The Hermit

We have all experienced this scenario – you read about someone who has written books in the same genre you are currently writing your first manuscript in, and she has already topped the bestseller charts, along with getting recommendations from everyone you admire, with exhortations of how brilliant and original her work is. You shut down the laptop and lie down on your bed – thinking how futile it all is – what is the point of toiling away at this rubbish manuscript when it will never get published, never be brilliant, never be endorsed by

Stephen King? You put away your manuscript, not turning to look at it for months, utterly disheartened.

This is why you must adopt the mind-set of **The Hermit**, at any time when the existence of your work is threatened. Harsh judgment, even from ourselves, can kill our creative spirit and prevent us from reaching our own potential, whatever that may be.

So I suggest a self-imposed break from reading about those in your field while you are working on creating the scaffolding of your work – lest you give up or feel tempted to take the safe, easy path, thus guaranteeing a rotten framework. If you are writing a mystery novel, by all means read non-fiction or romance novels, but stay away from writer's interviews or writer blogs. You don't want to stumble on a guest post by a bestselling writer on how she wrote her novel in three weeks while looking after her newborn baby. It will just make you miserable.

Invest your limited energy and resources into fleshing out your work-in-progress, and don't let your peers' multi-million dollar deals sway you. Become a hermit and stay away from any media that could destroy your desire to work at your art.

The Apprentice

I can hear your protests – surely hiding like an ostrich will not help our careers, don't we have to network and shouldn't I be learning tips from those successful in my field? Yes, it is true that we have a lot to learn from our peers and betters. And there is a stage for that – when not only will you learn from others, but you have full permission to spend hours on [insert favorite website here] researching the hacks and work habits of the leading lights in your field.

That stage is the revision stage. Whether you just wrote a screenplay, a novel or a business book, once you have put the basic parts down, you need to revise and edit. And this is when you will benefit most from external input. Maybe you can get tips to improve your dialogue. Or ideas on structuring your prose more coherently. With something concrete in hand, when you read about those in your field succeeding, there is less envy and more "how-can-I-do-that-too". You feel inspired to go back to your creation, maybe having gained a fresh perspective – which is really crucial at this stage. However, doing this when you have yet to complete your work-in-progress, you are much more likely to give up in frustration seeing all the ways your precious idea-baby is lacking.

So to recap – if you are still in the throes of putting together your first draft, close your browser, open up your project document and get going. Don't look left or right – till you have something that can be revised and improved. Don't think about the prizes and book sales others may be getting, or how badly or well your work will be perceived.

Once you have something to work with, become a sponge and soak up all the knowledge you can. **Apprentice** yourself to anyone you admire – learning from their work habits or their output, and go back to your own creation and see how you can make it better.

For now, I'm off to be a hermit myself.

29

OVERCOMING THE EGO: CREATING A BODY OF WORK

As writers we would like to believe that each book we work on is a "heartbreaking work of staggering genius", but even if that is the case, it isn't always easy to convince others of that fact. There are so many choices for readers, not to mention the competing sources of entertainment such as TV, movies and games for their leisure time, which makes it hard to ensure that your wonderful book will get the attention it deserves.

Perhaps as an artist, one should ignore the facts of readership and focus simply on writing. Or you may believe that luck is all that you need to ensure that your books sell. Or maybe, you obsess over your sales stats, letting your mood get affected by whether sales are up or down.

There is an idea that some authors and other creatives believe, that may sound slightly heretical. Here it is: Just keep doing your creative work, putting it out there and going on to the next idea in the queue. Write a book, release it and then start writing the next one. It's a pragmatic, craftsman-like approach to creativity. When I think of this concept, the idea of a carpenter comes to mind - one who works daily on a piece of furniture, finishes it and starts the next one. Whether the first few pieces sold well doesn't deter him from creating the next one, and being sold out probably would just spur him on to work harder.

This is a very different idea from the myth of the tortured artist, of working when the mood strikes, keeping the world at bay. I have to admit I bought into this myth for a long time, and I still find it hard to fully brush it off. Sometimes I find myself sitting down to work by the clock, and some days, when my mind is foggy, and the work isn't coming together, I want to buy into the notion that the muse isn't visiting today, and maybe I'm just not in the mood.

I have noticed this coincides with times when my ego is more intensely involved in my work than usual. Perhaps I'm getting closer to the completion point - when I will soon be judged on the work, and I am not sure about the reaction. Sometimes it happens when my books are selling well, and I want to bask in the myth of being a genius who works when the mood strikes, and not a worker who watches the clock and puts in the hours. Often it happens when I have started to overthink the work, what it might achieve, how it might be perceived. Days when I put all that behind me, and just focus on editing this chapter, this page, this paragraph, and shut out the rest of the world, the muse is whispering in my ear and the work flies along. Those are the days I have managed to quiet the ego.

Anne Lamott called this looking at a "one-inch picture frame". You just focus on the tiniest bit of the patchwork, forgetting the pattern of the quilt. When I'm thinking about my work as a whole, I find the anxieties and worries about the work overtake my creativity and I become stuck. When I focus on just that one-inch, I can shut all that out. I can shut the ego out.

I am struggling right now to complete a bunch of projects that I have started at various times and not finished. It's hard, because my ego wants every project to be perfect, wants me to think about every project as if it is the only one I will ever write. How will it be perceived? What will people say about it? Will it be talked about on social media?

When I manage to quiet down the ego I realize, what I am after is a body of work, not one perfect limb. I want to wait for reactions after I have completed what is in front of me, in fact, worrying about reactions will prevent me from completing it. The work should be the key, not how it is perceived. Not right now, while I still have a lot to learn, and each project is helping me grow hugely as a writer. I can't afford to stop that learning while I posture and preen for the readers, whether there are few or many.

This daily struggle reminds me that the difficulty of being a writer is not in learning to string words together, it is doing it despite your internal drama, and doing it consistently.

30

BE GOOD OR GETTING BETTER?

A book by psychologist Heidi Grant Halvorson on achieving goals surprisingly has some useful lessons for writers.

In her book *Succeed: How We Can Reach Our Goals*, psychologist Dr. Halvorson writes about two ways of thinking about setting goals – *be good* or *getting better*. "Be good" goals are about proving ourselves, while "getting better" goals are about improving ourselves. The way we set the goal influences how we approach the goal, and whether we succeed in achieving it. It also influences our level of stress and the journey we take towards making the goal happen.

All of this is very abstract, so I will try to give a concrete example. Let's say you are working on a book, your first novel. You get an idea and you are excited to begin. Then as you are writing, you notice that it's no longer flowing as well, you seem to keep getting stuck. You write a scene and then compare that scene to your favorite books in that genre and fall short. You start to question yourself – "Whatever made me think I could be a writer? I am just kidding myself!" You are stressed out and irritable. Your family is secretly hoping you give up on this dream of being a writer if this is how you will behave the whole time. You wonder what you're doing wrong, and go on forums that talk about writer's block and read quotes about the difficulty of being a writer.

What is really going on is that you're approaching your writing from a *be good* perspective. You want your book to be good, after all who doesn't, and you are mentally comparing your performance of writing with that of successful, published authors, and seeing yourself falling short constantly.

Now let's see another way to approach this. You sit down to write your first novel, excited, but aware that you probably have a lot to learn. You didn't take any fiction writing courses in college. So all you have is a story or the beginning of one, and a trusty laptop. You start writing and come to a point where the story breaks down, or it feels like every word you're typing is the wrong one. You ask yourself what you're doing wrong. Then you realize - this is your *first* novel. It couldn't possibly be that great from the first draft, or that easy to write. You decide to pause and get some books on craft, and devour them. Maybe you take an online writing course with a good instructor.

Now with some knowledge, you get back to your book. And you realize that while it's still hard, at least you now have a basic idea about setting and characterization and plot. You have a good idea of where this story is going. You can see that already you have improved so much. And you decide that no matter how terrible the writing is, you will power through and finish a draft, even if it's very rough. And you do. The whole time reminding yourself that it is a first novel, your first draft, and allowed to be terrible. You have some sleepless nights wondering if you can get to the end, but by and large you are not too stressed out. You even smile and laugh on occasion. You tell people about this crazy thing you are doing as an experiment, just to see where it will lead.

At the end of a few months of hard work, you have a rough

draft of your novel. And then you go back to those books on craft, and revise the whole thing. Pulling out scenes ruthlessly, working on the motivations of your characters, agonizing over every word choice. You can see through this process, that no matter how hard it is, the book is getting better. And you are improving as a writer with every hour you spend. This is how you tackle writing with a *getting better* perspective.

Notice some differences? Notice that both writers start with the same overall goal - to write a first novel. But the first writer wants their work to be instantly good, to be comparable with that of seasoned authors who have honed their craft over millions of words. While it may sound silly, it's surprisingly common for beginner writers to think this way. In fact, I fall for the same wrong-headed thinking myself. While working on a book of personal essays, I started reading a funny memoir by writer Jennifer Weiner tiled *Hungry Heart*. I haven't really read many of her books, but this one is really good. So good that I wasn't able to get back to working on my own book, because I was so deflated comparing her writing style to my own and falling short. But I forgot, until I wrote this post, that Jennifer Weiner has many best-selling books under her belt, and many more years of writing than me. I should aspire to be a good writer, even a great one. But I shouldn't let that aspiration for tomorrow stop me from putting down the words today.

Be good is a great goal for certain situations. If you have practiced a musical instrument for years and are going on stage to perform, by all means have your goal be to be as good as you possibly can. Aim to give a flawless performance. But if you are walking into dance class or acting class or a poetry writing seminar for the first time, or you are attempting to learn a new skill, then approach it with an attitude of *getting better*. Aim to learn, to improve, to start wherever you are and build from there.

If you are a newbie writer, by all means look up to your

writing heroes for inspiration. But don't forget to come back down to earth, and remember that you starting with a different mound of clay than them, and you don't yet have a seasoned potter's practiced hand. That is however no excuse to fear the clay - work with it, make it your own, put in the time. And maybe one day you will even be sitting right next to one of those experts, working the clay with the same level of confidence and skill. And your finished pots will be just as beautiful.

31

____

THE CREATIVITY MYTH

I have always wanted to be a writer, and I just assumed that eventually as I grew up, along with everything else I did, I would write. Regularly. And get published.

And yet, I didn't realize as I grew older, that I had absorbed some myths about writing. I believed that I had to wait for some mythic inspiration to strike before I was able to put words to paper. I thought I was supposed to wait for the words to magically appear in my mind, not knowing that simply sitting at the computer typing would get me far further than "waiting" for the muse while I watched TV or played games. In my case, I expected the muse to break down the door with a sledgehammer, because even when inspiration regularly knocked, I neglected to write down the snippets that it passed under the door. I sometimes got entire paragraphs of text, and ignored them, let them go. In retrospect, I have no clue what I was waiting for. For a neon sign inviting me to sit down to write. Or some wise person to give me a stirring speech about fate and destiny.

I guess I thought writing stories was very different from writing research papers. With the latter, you did research, typed up some tentative thoughts, moved paragraphs around, did some more research, and cobbled together a piece. With Art, on the other hand, you sat at the pad or computer, and someone whispered in your ear, and you simply wrote swathes of beautiful prose, tidied up the grammar a bit, and voila, you had a manuscript. And since that never happened to me, I never completed anything. I started many things, but since they didn't flow completely in one session, I never bothered to complete them. I guess I thought talent was something divine, not something you can hone.

Over the past year however, I have slowly realized that what makes you a writer is this – the willingness to write down everything that occurs to you, trying to move words around so that they make some sort of sense, putting your ideas and stories out there without being precious about it. Putting in the effort to make something the best you can and then simply letting it go. Experience. Patience. A bit of luck. This is what turns you into a writer.

The process isn't too different from the way I write non-fiction or academic articles. I put down all the words I can think of, in all the combinations I can think of. Then I delete the parts that don't make any sense, move things around, revise as much as I can. I spend hours trying to shape the piece, and a lot of the time it feels like I am trying to wedge the wrong pieces of a puzzle together because I just can't be bothered anymore. I put the sky piece next to the grass piece and then call it a day. But then when I come back to it later, after I have revised the piece so many times that I can't look at it anymore, the sky and grass pieces somehow seem to fit. The writing flows, the structure works, the words make sense.

In my current work-in-progress, I just couldn't find a way to put down the words. I wanted to circle back to the same scenes, the same emotional truths over and over. Seeing that as a fatal flaw in my writing process, I simply stopped working, hoping that magically one day I would know exactly what to write, how to fill in the gaps. Perhaps what I needed instead was to write the same scene over and over in various ways. I have since read about writers, both contemporary and classical, who have experienced this same feeling of going around and around in circles, like a dog chasing its tail. Maybe I should have kept at it, and it would have helped me to settle down into my work; which is really what the dog is doing as well, evolutionarily programmed to make its grassy bed.

I read a blog post by science fiction author and blogger Jamie Todd Rubin, in which he described his writing method: he first writes one draft telling the story to himself, and a second draft where he tells the story to his readers. It's such a simple and yet powerful way of breaking down the writing process. Reading this reinforced the idea that my myth of the writer effortlessly breezing through the story from beginning to end in chronological order, with all plot twists and turns neatly worked out in one fell swoop was, just that, a myth. Writers get the kernel of an idea, and then they must work hard at it, to turn that kernel into a crackling good tale.

This probably applies to endeavors beyond just writing, or even broader than art. I imagine that students might believe that *successful* students sail through the examination in chronological order, when in reality many, myself included, jump back and forth between easy and difficult questions, answering as much as possible. A finished presentation may look seamless, but from experience I know that the execution is often patchy and chaotic, everything falling into place at the last minute. Sometimes all you can do is make whatever little progress you can, setting up a cumulative effect that builds on itself.

Maybe creativity isn't a flashy designer, with bolts of silk, fashioning a garment from large pieces of cloth. Maybe creativity more closely resembles a weaver, weaving a complex tapestry from small pieces of thread, intertwined over time into a material that absorbs the individual fibers, into a seamless design.

32

LEARNING TO FAIL

One insight that artists and creative professionals could learn from the world of business is the importance of being willing to fail. After all, the way to get better at our craft involves trying different things, often trying something that is out of our comfort zone in an area where we haven't fully developed our skill, and seeing what works.

Entrepreneurs have a useful mindset that we can borrow – they "move fast and break things", they ship out a product that is still in "beta testing" and they simply release newer versions with some "bugs" fixed (and presumably others not yet found or fixed). The entrepreneurial mindset has comfort with failure built into it, probably due in some part to the high rates of failure of many kinds of businesses.

However, as artists, it is not always easy to allow ourselves to fail, or even to entertain the possibility of failure. Especially when you are trying to establish yourself, your mind fills with doubts and doomsday scenarios - this current project will bomb, you will metaphorically fall on your face and no one will ever buy your art. Ironically, the one thing you need to do to get better, is what you often feel incapable of doing.

So if you cannot eagerly sign yourself up for failure, what do you do then?

While working on one of my non-fiction books, I really struggled with the book's structure. I had misgivings about the flow and whether it was innovative enough and well-researched enough. I got panicky thinking that I didn't know what I was doing, and I should just quit. After all the hours I put into it I couldn't bear to simply give up, but I didn't know what else to do.

I was afraid to fail. I was afraid of giving up, and yet I was afraid that if I went through with it in its current form, my work would be terrible and I would look amateurish. I was stuck and miserable.

And then I asked myself what would be the worst thing that happened if I did an average job. It wouldn't be failing exactly, but I wouldn't be killing it either. And I realized that it wouldn't be that bad. I gave myself permission to be average, which really meant giving myself permission to fail.

I started over, and within very little time I had a new outline. And this is the strange part - it was actually much better than the previous one, and looked much more professional than I was expecting. I was actually really happy with it.

In a way, letting myself fail didn't actually lead to failure (well right away anyway). What it did do was free myself up to be more creative, to look at the problem from a different angle, one that I wouldn't have considered otherwise.

So, to come back to the question, if you can't eagerly sign up for failure, how do you gain the ability to learn from it?

Think about that project that you abandoned, or haven't finished despite numerous attempts, because you were trying to get it just right. Think about that idea that you had but were too afraid to try in case you got it completely wrong. These are projects that you've already doomed to the dust heap, because you think they are a lost cause. Pick one of these projects up and give yourself permission to do an average job. At least it will get done. And you will learn the valuable lesson of learning from failure. You may even fail to success, as prolific author Dean Wesley Smith says. What do you have to lose?

What is the fear of failure holding you back from accomplishing?

33

DELIBERATE PRACTICE AND BECOMING A SUCCESSFUL WRITER

The Myth of Talent

Noted psychologist Anders Ericsson's book *Peak: Secrets From The New Science of Expertise* has a lot of insights from it that are especially applicable to writers and other creatives. While the book focuses a lot on elite athletes and performers, and the techniques that help them get to that level and beyond, I think it is equally helpful for anyone wanting to be a writer or painter or film director, starting out and wondering how to achieve their dream.

I don't discount the role of luck and fortune and timing in achieving success for those in the arts. Not every talented person will make it. Not every book will be a bestseller, or every deserving movie get an award. But what about all those people whose heart is set on writing a novel and getting it published, but they keep getting rejected? Or those who want to paint or learn a musical instrument, perhaps just as a hobby, but fear that since they didn't start as a child, it is too late for them to pick it up? Or maybe they just believe they lack the "talent" for whatever pursuit they aim for?

The word *talent* itself can be quite misleading. It's always bothered me ever since I read the book *The Talent Code* by Daniel Coyle and realized how much of what we think of as miraculous, innate ability is simply the result of hours of hard work and practice. *Peak* underscores this notion. The skills of elite musicians and athletes and mathematicians can be attributed to years of focused practice that honed their skills and abilities, which an outsider often tends to attribute to some magical quality that they must have been born with. There is however no gene that selected people come into the world with, that enables them to become chess grandmasters or golf pros or tennis champions. Even Mozart practiced for years before he became a truly original composer of classical music.

But What About Twilight?

Unfortunately, the world of publishing is quite different, at least from the outside, from the world of Olympic athletes and Carnegie Hall concert pianists. While you wouldn't expect someone who started playing the piano three months ago to perform at the world's best venues, or a gymnast with six months of training to make the Olympic team, we routinely hear of debut authors whose book hit the New York Times list or has sold a million copies.

Which is why, whenever I read research that debunks the myth of talent, a small voice in my head would pipe up – "But what about *Twilight*? And *50 Shades of Grey*? And the *Harry Potter* series?"

There may be debate about the quality of some of the books that make it to bestseller status, but I believe (and am not alone in this belief) that J.K. Rowling's bestseller series are some of the best books I have read, with obvious mastery of the craft of storytelling. How did a first-time author write something so inventive and original?

According to profiles on the authors whose books I admire, many of them actually did write for years before their most famous work hit the bestseller lists - either with previously published books that went under the radar, or writing for years before being published. In other cases, the first book showed promise, but subsequent books in the series or by the same author improved significantly, showing that the author got better as a writer with each novel under her belt.

And of course, there is a whole host of other factors, such as timing, savvy marketing and the fact that many really good books don't get the spotlight they deserve. That is a problem of the arts, where you can't rank every author or painter in the way you can with athletes or chess players.

There is, however, one lesson that stood out in all my reading, and the primary takeaway for me from *Peak*. No matter where your talent level currently lies, you can get better with practice. With the right kind of practice.

The Promise of Deliberate Practice

Without giving a lecture on the subject, the definition of *deliberate practice* or the kind of practice that Ericsson claims improves skill at a fast pace, is that you work on improving specific aspects of the skill, with full concentration, working just outside your comfort zone. The essential components are that you identify your weaknesses, find ways to practice to improve them and get feedback so that you know whether you are getting better or closer to the desired outcome.

For writing fiction, that might mean choosing a specific aspect of craft to hone, such as writing more compelling characters, and revising your manuscript or writing a fresh story where you specifically aim to improve your characterization.

You read craft books and take writing courses that help you get to the next level.

While this is generally something most authors aspire to anyway, a student of deliberate practice might make it an integral part of their approach. They might constantly seek feedback (from teachers, trusted readers, other authors) to hone in on their weaknesses as storytellers and seek to address them one at a time in each upcoming story. They might take courses specifically targeted to whichever aspects of storytelling they feel they need to beef up. They never get comfortable, always taking on a harder and harder challenge, pushing the boundaries of what they are capable of.

I believe that this approach can help a veteran author of ten novels as much as a beginner thinking about their first. Many more people want to write fiction than actually attempt it, and I think a big part of it is due to this myth about talent. When I tell people that I am working on a book, most people wistfully tell me they would love to write, if only they had the talent. For many this wish might be on par with me wishing I could sing better, even though I am not ready to sign up for singing lessons and devote three evenings a week to practicing scales. But others might be harboring a strong, secret desire to write, but are held back by the belief that they don't have the talent.

No matter where you are as a writer, you can improve. Sometimes when we see amazing art out in the world, incredibly well-made movies or books that stay with you long after you close the page or plays that bring those who never watched a play into the theatre, we think that the person who created this couldn't possibly be someone like me. I couldn't possibly do anything as beautiful as this. As I watched the Academy Awards recently with tears streaming down my face, I was inspired by the diverse range and strength of talent on display. But I reminded myself that all of them had started out, nervous and unsure, facing the camera or the blank page for the first time, and put in years of dedicated effort to get where they are today. And while our efforts may not guarantee us an Oscar, my understanding of deliberate practice convinces me that steady effort at my craft will guarantee that I too can look back years later, and be amazed at the difference in the quality of my work. The years go by one way or the other. I would rather that I spent them aiming for something just outside my grasp, even if I never quite reached it, than wishing that I had had the courage to try.

So in the words of Benj Pasek and Justin Paul (*La La Land*):
"Here's to the ones who dream,
Foolish as they may seem".

34

STEPPING OUT OF THE SHADOWS

I have been reading books on the art and craft of writing ever since I found a whole shelf of them in the British Council library in New Delhi at the age of fourteen. I would bring home books on dialogue, setting, narrative and characters. I read articles on writing query letters and doing research and getting an agent - all the traditional aspects of being a writer, before the advent of indie publishing. I read every book I could get my hands on, and yet almost never wrote anything myself. I didn't believe that anyone would want to read anything I had to say, in fact, I believed that I didn't really have anything to say. I was what Julia Cameron calls, a "shadow writer".

Sure, I wrote essays in school for assignments and tests. I got back my English exams with glowing praise on the margins of my essays - I remember one comment from my English teacher, someone I particularly adored and respected - she had said "It's a pleasure to read your writing, as always!" I loved the praise, and yet couldn't bring myself to believe it. She was just being nice, I told myself. I entered competitions in school for essays, and won certificates. And yet I continued to believe that

I wasn't any good at writing - after all, if I had been, I would have won first prize. I was waiting for external validation, a stamp that told me I was a writer, and that now I had permission to create. And yet I rejected every form of validation that I did happen to receive, as not being glowing enough, or not conclusive enough to "prove" my writing talent.

By the time I graduated high school, I had an idea at the back of my mind that one day I would write books, and be a "real writer", but that it would be something I did along with my primary career. It never occurred to me that I could ever earn a living solely by writing, or that I would want to. By this time, I had stopped asking myself whether I could write, but I still wasn't writing anything that wasn't assigned in school.

In college, I started to rub up against the writing life by fantasizing about writing freelance articles, and collected writer's guidelines for magazines like the way some people collect stamps. I carefully filed them away and dreamt of the articles I could be writing, deluding myself that just one of these days I would get around to actually writing something.

In the meantime, I had been commissioned by an Indian publisher to write a study guide on the poems of Seamus Heaney. I was thrilled, working on the book while juggling law school and being involved in every college activity I had any talent in, but still I wasn't able to think of myself as a writer, published or otherwise. I tried to get a gig writing reviews for the arts section of the campus newspaper, but the editor seemed to hate the one review I wrote for him, and never asked me back. That one rejection did more to convince me that I couldn't write (and couldn't ever hope to) than all the compliments I had received over the years made me think I could.

It was only years later, when I came across a yellow book in a bookstore while browsing the writing reference section, that I finally had the courage to put words on paper without waiting for an external assignment. Julia Cameron's book *The Right to*

Write gave me the tools to tentatively explore writing without expectations. Although it was predictably rocky going, at least I had begun.

In another book, *The Artist's Way*, Cameron first mentions the notion of "shadow artists", who desperately want to make art but are afraid, so they instead try to stay close to their chosen medium in various ways, while lacking the courage to actually create art themselves. I realized this is what I had been doing for years - reading books about writing, even when I wasn't writing anything myself. And when I finally did start to write, I almost gave up just as soon, because those writing books filled my head as I tentatively put down one word after another - I started to think about how difficult it was to get an agent or write a good query letter or how writers got hundreds of rejection letters before they sold anything. I was putting the cart before the horse - worrying about publishing before I had finished a single piece of writing.

It took me years to tentatively come out of the shadows, and actually start creating my own art. Last year I published three books. This is my thirteenth book. And yet when people ask me what I do, I can't bring myself to tell them that I am a writer. When I was writing full-time, it took me a while, but I finally became comfortable enough about my writing to actually speak about in public. When I was at an event where people asked me what I do, I began to tentatively declare – "I write books". The reactions were varied, and some people showed a lot of interest. I found myself hesitatingly explaining what my current book was about.

Since I began my current job in a consulting firm, it became a lot easier to simply tell people that I was a consultant. Did I make the shift for expediency, or without really thinking about it had I stepped back into the shadows? As I have been editing this book, I have been thinking more about this issue. Recently, over lunch with a new colleague, when asked what I do outside work, I said "I write books", and this time, I did not hesitate. My colleague was interested and asked questions, and I felt comfortable responding unhesitatingly.

Although I may not constantly talk about my work-in-progress or share my writing with everyone, I realize that I'm no longer in the shadows, cowering. I stepped out, and decided, however shakily, that I would claim my identity as a "real artist", as a writer. I might find it hard to always claim my title, but at least I no longer need to covet my art from a distance. I write, and regardless of the quality of each individual piece, as the work piles up, I know that my artist self is an integral part of my life.

35

THE POSITIVE GIFT OF CREATIVITY

Last night I was watching the [2017] BAFTA awards, which had many funny and interesting and nostalgic moments. But a couple of speeches really stood out for me.

The first was actress Emma Stone's speech on receiving her BAFTA for Best Actress (for *La La Land*). She spoke about the positive gift of creativity, and how it can make a difference, especially when times are hard. Many of the other recipients spoke in the same vein, including the movie's producers, about how important it is for filmmakers to keep producing art, and to keep giving us experiences on screen that remind us of our shared humanity.

Around this same time, I was reading this book by psychologist Anders Ericsson titled *Peak*. And among the many things I learned from this book, was this giant insight (this wasn't technically written in the book, but the pieces fell into place while reading it) – that I need to write and keep writing, and with each story, I will become a better writer. Now this seems so obvious, until I parse this out a bit more.

I am working on (or rather am supposed to be working on)

revising my first novel to publish it. I am putting it off and not working on it, because I am scared that it's not very good. Which is quite likely since this is my first novel. And yet, the point of writing it and putting it out there is not so that I can put out a great novel. Because that's not very likely, right off the bat. The point is to become a better writer. I will become better just through the act of writing and finishing. And with each story I write and publish, I will get even better. And one day, maybe not too far away in the future, I will write a story that will remind those who read it of our shared humanity. And make them cry or laugh or both.

I believe in the power of art. I always have. But at the same time, I don't believe in the power of *my* art. I don't think that I can write all that well, and the more scared I am, the less likely I am to do the work, the work that will make me a *better* writer.

On one hand, I put Art on a pedestal. Art with a capital A - everything that is beautiful, moving, full of emotion. But in order to be an artist, with a small a, one has to remove some of that power. One has to claim that power for oneself. No one becomes an artist, small or big, successful or otherwise, in one day, with one piece. You have to hone your craft, no matter how much talent you are born with. And being afraid to experiment, being afraid to play, that stops you from developing your craft and honing your talent.

Although this is easy to say, it is difficult to do. Fear stops us. Fear gets in our head, telling us that we are stupid to even think of writing a book, painting a portrait, performing a play or whatever. How do we stop that fear? I've read lots of books and tried lots of techniques that claim to have an answer, but at the heart of it all is just one thing - love.

I know I know - corny. But as I am writing this on Valentine's Day, maybe you can indulge me for a moment. Remember why you wanted to create the art in the first place – whether it is to write, paint, sing or act. Remember what it feels like to watch a performance, see a painting, read a story that mesmerizes you. And for the love of that feeling, go for it. It is important to love the people in our life and to express that love, but I think it is just as important to love our art, our creativity. To love the fruits of that creative expression, no matter how rough-hewn and unpolished for the moment. And I believe that for the love affair with your art to count, you have to nurture that love, give it time and patience and loving care, spending every moment you can steal with it. Like Elizabeth Gilbert says, have a love affair with your creativity. And watch it love you back.

36

____

MINDSET AND CREATIVITY

While researching my book on study skills I came across this fantastic book called *Mindset*. It's written by renowned Stanford University psychologist Dr. Carol Dweck, and reading the book changed the way I saw a lot of things. It definitely had a huge impact on the way I presented and wrote my book.

I was reminded of this book recently because I have been reading *Succeed: How We Can Reach Our Goals* by Dr. Heidi Grant Halvorson, coincidentally a mentee and colleague of Dr. Dweck. While reading her book I was thinking a lot about the struggles I faced recently with my writing and other goals, and decided to write down and share some of my insights (at least those regarding writing) in case they prove useful to other writers.

One of the big takeaways for me from the book *Mindset* was that there are two ways of looking at challenges and goals. One is that of the *fixed mindset* - where you are more concerned with how you appear to others and with proving something - that you are smart (in the context of school) or that you are a good writer. The other attitude is that of a *growth mindset* - where you are more interested in learning or improving, and even when something is hard, you persevere because you want to master the subject. And the author gives lots of examples, how you would approach goals differently based on what mindset you have.

And this is the crux - as a writer or creative person, we know this, we have heard it a 100 times - you need to keep learning, you need to keep trying, put in the 10,000 hours of practice.

The fact is, however, that once you get to a certain level of competence, if you are in the fixed mindset, you may not want to rock the boat by taking on a challenge where you might not succeed, when you would appear to have failed. This is devastating to a person with that mindset, at least where their writing is concerned (I believe that we have different attitudes in different arenas and at different stages in life). This would mean that this person would only take on writing projects they are inherently good at, or far more commonly, they would experience writer's block and not be able to write anything. Not because they literally cannot write, but because everything that comes out is clunky or terrible (because they can't write that sort of book yet, but they don't want to think about that). The fixed mindset writer wants to appear to be a good writer, so bad writing throws them off.

And this can differ from project to project, maybe even day to day. I realized that I have been experiencing this issue of mindset with one of the projects I am blocked on. I am attempting to write a book of humorous essays. I love reading books of humorous essays myself, and have huge respect and awe for writers who can pull them off successfully. As a result, I am stuck on my own book. The first few essays were ok, because somehow it seemed fun and a lark. But then it finally hit me that I am writing the book, that I am making progress towards it, and then I started to get stuck. Nothing was good.

There was no humor. I was comparing my work to the best authors, the ones whose books I loved. Clearly I couldn't hold a candle to them. So even though I desperately wanted to finish the book, I couldn't get out a word.

Then I realized that this is what I was doing. I was trying to prove (not sure to whom, since I haven't showed the work to anyone) that I was a good humor writer. And this is absurd since I have never written humor before. I can't possibly be good right away. But I so badly wanted to be. Then I decided that I would lower my standards - focus on learning how to do it, on writing a crappy first draft and using it as my canvas to experiment. I would get advice on writing funny essays and try to see how to apply this within my book. Even if I didn't get to any great level, I would have improved and maybe learnt some techniques I could apply elsewhere in my writing.

I am still hoping that the book does come out to be good and that people like it, but I realize that trying to prove that I was good right off the bat would most likely result in not having a book. (*Update:* I did finish the book and at least some people seemed to like it and find it funny, which was enough for me.)

So, this is my little two cents of advice - no matter where you are in your creativity / writing journey, ask yourself if you're trying mostly to learn or mostly to prove yourself. There will be elements of both, but too much of trying to prove yourself results in sticking to things you absolutely know you can knock out of the park and stops further growth. In extreme cases, it also results in you not enjoying your work as much, and feeling too much pressure instead of enjoyment, which defeats the entire purpose.

What's your mindset when it comes to your writing? Can you approach your current project from a growth mindset?

37

THE POWER OF ART

This past week has been so terrible that sometimes I wonder whether thinking about what books to read or write or talking about how to become a better artist is shallow and pointless and meaningless. (*I initially wrote this chapter after a mass shooting event in the US, but am revising it during the global pandemic, which gave us more than a year's worth of devastating news*).

I studied law and public policy at university, and I care deeply about these topics. But at the same time, I find them depressing and disheartening. Not that I have run away from such topics, or don't read about them anymore - in fact the book I am revising right now is about the ban on cluster munitions, and full of depressing statistics about victims and landmines and the death of innocent people going about their everyday life. I am writing this book in the hope that I can spread even a small amount of awareness about the landmark ban on these weapons and encourage countries who haven't signed it to adopt the convention.

However, I am under no illusions that this is a niche topic. Not too many people are interested in cluster munitions. I know that is obvious, but it only became crystal clear to me when I told people what I was working on and noted their reaction - eyes glazed, polite smile and crab-like scuttle towards the nearest exit. This isn't the most scintillating topic to most people.

Not the case about the events of this week and generally the last few months. Most people have an opinion about gun control (or the lack thereof) and terrorism. Most people have the same opinions as me actually, in that most people don't approve of the murder of innocent people, no matter who they are. Which means that they would be interested in cluster munitions too - if they knew that in many countries, for instance during the Vietnam War, 30% or almost one-third of the millions of these bombs that were dropped into the Mekong region, did not detonate on impact, instead remaining for decades just waiting for an unsuspecting child or villager to come across, and get injured or killed.

Don't worry, this entire chapter is not about cluster munitions. In fact, I hadn't planned to mention them at all, but then I realized it was a perfect metaphor for what I really wanted to talk about.

The importance of story.

The power of art.

As I said, I worried that maybe I care too much about superficial things, like how many people read my books, and how many words I have managed to write. When far worse things are happening around the world. And then I realized - that the way people are wired, it is hard for us to care about all the terrible things that are happening all at once. Or to understand the impact of every bad thing that happens - every time a bomb goes off killing hundreds in (fill in the blank here) or gunfire is directed at (kids, people on the street, in a cafe, in a theater). Or to comprehend what we need to do to stop these terrible things from happening. People complain that the

Western media is selective - the deaths of two Europeans or five Americans are highlighted, but the hundreds of thousands of Africans that die of disease or poverty, or the Asian children that suffer from child labor and sweatshops and myriad other problems go unnoticed. While that may be slightly true, I think there is room enough for us to care about all the people who suffer - regardless of where they come from.

But the reality is that we don't. Some tragedies get more press and eyeballs and attention than others. And that matters because that determines where the attention for solutions go to as well. And this is even more stark for me, as I work on this book, because one of the reasons that the issue of cluster munitions, and landmines before it, got enough attention for the weapons to be banned, was that articles were written about them in the media, and powerful politicians and influential civil society organizations banded together to create change.

And it all started with something simple.

It started with a story.

And this is the point of this post. What can we as writers and authors and artists of all stripes do in the face of such horror and tragedy? We can create art. We can create stories.

They are powerful enough to heal when we are hurting. We can escape into a movie or a book, and forget our problems, forget the pain for a while. When I struggled with periods of loneliness and depression in college, I often resorted to a frothy chic-lit book to escape my issues for the evening - my favorite author and a bar of chocolate. While that contributed to my waistline, it also helped me get through that period and to the other side.

I am editing this book during the great pandemic of 2020, when the way most of us got through that year was by escaping into stories – what movies and TV shows on our favorite streaming service we were watching was what we talked about during our Zoom Monday morning meetings and Friday virtual happy hours.

So stories can make us feel better, make us feel happier.

When we go to the museum and see paintings full of emotion, depth, mastery of technique and color, we feel awe and see the beauty of not just the piece of art, but of the human race. We feel connected to something bigger than us, something eternal, something primal. And that is the power of art.

I want to revisit what I wrote earlier - what can we as writers or authors do? We actually have a lot more power than we know. And as Uncle Ben said to Peter Parker, "with great power comes great responsibility". As writers, we have the power to get the attention of people, to get their emotions involved in the world that we create, to make them see something from a completely different point of view than before.

I read somewhere that Princess Diana's involvement with the landmine ban campaign was the PR equivalent of a $2million campaign. Why was that? I was quite young then and don't remember the campaign, but I bet it was because she helped shape a specific story - focusing on the human costs of using these bombs. The campaign focused on the people who were affected, telling a story that was picked up by news media all over the world, and contributing to a landmark treaty banning anti-personnel mines.

I don't have any ideas about how to stop the violence. I don't know what really goes on in the head of someone who decides to deliberately take the life of another, especially the life of someone they don't know, have never met. Someone who hasn't harmed them in any way. But I do know that stories are powerful. We may not be running countries and deciding public policy. But we can affect change in subtle but powerful ways. In the stories we choose to tell. In the way we frame the issues.

I know that if I tell someone that I wrote a book about how a particular weapon was banned, they fall asleep talking to me.

But what if I told them instead that my book was about how people were needlessly dying from a war that ended decades earlier? Or that it was a classic David versus Goliath story - how a small group of countries and some passionate individuals managed to change defense policy and destroy millions of weapons that were a core part of the arsenal of the biggest military powers in the world?

What if we changed the stories told about climate change? About terrorism? About gun control? About racism and sexism and all the other ways that we hate each other and distrust each other and fail to live and work together in peace?

Like I said, I don't have all the answers, I don't have any answers to these big puzzling issues. But I have confidence in the power of one of the oldest vehicles of knowledge in the world. We already have stories about these issues - but in many cases those stories are no longer serving our highest good. Maybe it is time to write some new ones?

38

DON'T HIDE YOUR BRUSHSTROKES

When I sit down to write, I only have a vague idea of what I want to write about. I type the first few sentences, and it all seems wrong. My fingers linger over the keyboard, and it is almost as if my brain stopped sending signals to them, they don't know what to do anymore. I don't get any ideas -I stare at the blank screen for a few seconds, minutes, whatever, and then decide that it is pointless. I give up, closing down the word document. To distract myself, I go online and see what other people are writing, or pick up one of my favorite books. Everything seems so well-structured, so seamless. It's hopeless, I tell myself. I will never really be a writer.

Does this feel familiar? Go ahead and substitute your favorite creative verb in place of "writing"-painting, designing, filmmaking. Everywhere around us, there are people making amazing masterpieces and directing breath-taking movies and creating products or images that dazzle. And why stop there? If you design apps, you can point to a dozen or more perfect apps, or if you want to start a company, you can get overwhelmed looking at the bevy of successful startups. Why even risk inevitable failure and humiliation, when the outcome is guaranteed- guaranteed to disappoint?

Every successful writer, film-maker, poet, painter and entrepreneur knows something that many beginners do not- that it takes a lot of sweat, cursing, trashing pages or throwing away of entire prototypes before something amazing is born. Films spend months in the editing room, software goes through several phases of beta testing, and books get edited multiple times, before the mainstream audience is allowed to experience (and judge) these products.

And yet, as a beginner, or even with some experience, we creatives (and I use that word loosely to describe anyone who is making something for the consumption of others) tend to compare our early and flawed work to the best work of the greats. And we aren't entirely to blame. How often do the greats show us their early and flawed work? In *The Artists' Way*, author and creativity coach Julia Cameron recounts that she had arranged (to the shocked horror of other academics) for some established film-makers to showcase their first films to her students, in order to show them the path from ordinary to exceptional.

In Kevin Ashton's *How To Fly A Horse*, he recounts the myth of Mozart, based on a letter that apparently proved Mozart's genius, which stated that entire compositions just came to him in a dream. In actuality, Mozart struggled and pored over his work, spending sleepless nights and countless days perfecting each arrangement.

And yet the myth of the genius artist, the scam that some people are able to sit down and effortlessly, or with very little agony or inefficiency, create works of extraordinary depth, is compelling and pervasive. One of my favorite Yeats' poems, *Adam's Curse*, reiterates this myth:

A line will take us hours maybe;
Yet if it does not seem a moment's thought,

Our stitching and unstitching has been naught.

THIS MYTH DOES us a great disservice. We believe that our little ideas or thoughts aren't good enough - they aren't big enough or sketched out enough. We believe that if a piece is very rough to start with, there is no way that it can end up being as polished as that of the work of our idols, the work we admire. We forget that every diamond started out as a rough, ugly stone, almost indistinguishable from cheap cut glass, except to an expert's eye. We think that until we can produce professional, polished work, we should just not try. We forget that only by making those amateurish short films, writing those hackneyed blog posts and creating those clunky apps can we get good enough to do better, to be better.

If only we knew that even the greats start with a rough sketch, a back of the napkin calculation, an outline that is abandoned and turned inside out and barely recognizable once the finished product is out there. This is a plea then, for all creators - please show us your torn-up half-baked ideas, initial sketches, and cliché-ridden copy so that we too can be inspired to follow with our own half-baked, on the way to slightly average, yet brimming with potential, projects. Please, don't hide your brushstrokes.

39

WHAT ADVICE WOULD YOU GIVE TO A 13 YEAR OLD?

The other day I met the daughter of a recent acquaintance, and she shared with me her deep desire to be a writer. A fiction writer to be precise. A little further digging - she wanted to write fantasy books. The problem? She was not doing well in her English assignments in school - she was getting bad grades and felt miserable, because she took it as a sign that she might not be able to become a writer after all.

I remember well this feeling, of thinking that doing badly in school means the death of one's ambition in a certain subject or field. I even wrote an entire book about it. But hearing it from a young person was strange - the argument sounded so obviously flawed to me. How can your grade when you are 13 determine whether you can successfully accomplish something at 30? Or 20? But this is how the human mind works. We aren't rational or logical, or perhaps we are *too* rational and logical, and just assume that whoever we are today defines all that we can be tomorrow.

I have been listening to *Big Magic* by Elizabeth Gilbert on audiobook, and it is fascinating. Something that struck me deeply was her section on Permission. With a capital P. In her view, it isn't necessary to go to school to get an MFA or to get further education in the arts. Definitely not necessary if it gets you into debt. You don't need it to become an artist, whatever that means for you. And although I know this intellectually, hearing it from a successful writer was so deeply freeing.

When a 13-year-old tells me that she is devastated by a grade in English class, I know in my bones that that is not a real obstacle to being a writer. At the same time however, I tell myself that perhaps *I* would be further along in my quest to become a novelist if I had taken some creative writing courses in college.

Why do I believe in different rules for her and myself? Well, for one, there is a difference in our ages. No grade is truly devastating at 13, not unless you use it as an excuse to completely give up. It is a different issue at 30. But then again, why should it be? What stops me from taking courses now if I so choose, or taking up writing fiction? Is there an age limit for writing? Definitely not.

And this comes back to the issue of permission. Somehow it is easier to give permission to someone else than to ourselves. It is easier for me to see that the possibilities are endless for a 13-year old. It is easier to think that she has the time ahead of her to take multiple paths and find the right one. That she has time to learn all that she needs to write the books she dreams of.

It is not so easy however, to give myself the same permission. To see that I have the same paths open to me as she does - just different entry points, different hurdles to step around, different flowers to admire. They might not even be of the same distance. But they lead us to the same destination - the realization that perhaps for those wanting to live a creative life, there isn't really a set end point, a set goal. We aren't all walking towards the same finish line. We aren't even running the same race. Some authors will write 20 books, finding a small but loyal audience. Others may write only one or two, but hit critical acclaim right away. Some will write many books or short stories or plays, only publishing a small percentage of their work. Some works will win prizes, others loyal fans, others will go unnoticed. It isn't a certain life, and definitely not one for the faint-hearted.

So then I come back to the question - what advice would I give that 13-year-old would-be writer? On the spur of the moment I did say some encouraging things, some platitudes and assurances. But now with hindsight what would I have liked to have said? That there is no set path for a writer. That while no one teacher's opinion can stop her from being a writer, there are in fact a hundred things that can stop her. Other people's opinions. Rejections. Other people's successes. Her own failures. Her own successes. Family. Life. And maybe this is what I should have said. If you really want to be a writer, nothing and no one can stop you. You don't need permission. You don't need perfect circumstances. You don't even need inspiration. All you need is a notebook, some reliable pens, a head full of stories and a heart full of love. Love for books and stories, and for the process of story-telling. However corny this sounds, you need love to transcend the fears and objections of the world. And these requirements are the same whether you are thirteen or thirty.

40

KEEP ON TRUCKIN'

I was reading some old blog posts of prolific author and blogger Dean Wesley Smith, and I came across a post about prolific fiction authors. As he noted, some of the authors on his list had published over 500 books, some over 1,000. Granted, many of these were collections of shorter works, or edited anthologies, but the fact remains that these authors wrote a lot in their lifetime.

I guess it is no coincidence that many of these names are household names and most of us have heard of them even if we haven't read their books - L. Ron Hubbard, Barbara Cartland, Isaac Asimov.

In the book *Originals* by Adam Grant, he writes that Beethoven had only a handful of "genius" level works, out of his total output of over 600 compositions. Shakespeare wrote 37 plays and dozens of sonnets, but only five or six are most familiar to us and deemed his best work. Picasso created an astonishing number (in the thousands) of paintings, sketches and sculptures, but only a few are the most sought after.

So the question is - did they become so successful and famous because they were really good, or were they really good because they were prolific? In other words, does quantity affect quality?

For some reason, this is a discussion my mom and I have very often. One of our favorite actors is Amitabh Bachchan, a stalwart in the Indian film industry. He has acted in hundreds of films, or at least so it seems. In many he was the leading man, but he has also taken supporting roles and performed brief cameos. Of those several dozen roles, only a handful leap out when we think of him. Some of his work is in fact, truly appalling; clearly roles he took when nothing else was on offer. However, the sum total of his work is what we admire, the fact that he was brilliant in certain roles, even when the rest of the movie had little to commend it.

How did he become brilliant though? Was he just born an exceptional actor? Some academics believe that a lot of what we think of as innate talent is really a measure of skill. Sure, you need some innate ability, some aptitude, but more often than not it simply stems from passion, interest and spending hours and hours on some activity while you get better and better. If I acted in a 100 films, I might be a pretty good actor. Of course, there is no guarantee that I would be great, but passably good definitely. Enough to create a career, and carve a niche for myself. The point is that you need to have the discipline and the interest in a creative pursuit to stick it out over time. And you need a way to get in the door.

Today, thanks to technology, getting in the door is a lot easier. We can create our own opportunities. We can write a book and self-publish it. We can take our iPhones, a few friends and some software, and create our own movie. We can upload that to Youtube, or try to get it shown at festivals. We can rent a space for a night and showcase our photographs or our artwork. To some extent, we can create our own breaks. The harder part is getting someone to care, to show up, to appreciate our work.

And maybe this is why we need to go for quantity - because as we keep putting our work out there, over time, there is a greater chance that it will get noticed. If I write one book, it might get lost in the sea out there. But if I write 30, the chances are someone will stumble on one, get excited about all the others and maybe read a large number of them. Maybe they will recommend them to a friend, or share their excitement on social media. That's how you get people to care.

And of course it doesn't hurt that writing 30 books will transform me as a writer. Perhaps my first or second or even tenth book isn't too good. But hopefully each one is much better than the other, hopefully I keep learning, and by the time I am at my 20th or 25th, they are pretty good. Good enough to be read by many people and enjoyed and hopefully open up many other opportunities related to writing for me.

And this is probably the strategy of anyone smart enough to see this trend. If you keep at it, you will inevitably get better. You will hone your craft and polish your prose and really fall in love with your work, whatever it is. And it won't matter whether you have the lead role or just a cameo. If you give your best to every part, every piece of art, over time you have a body of work to be proud of. And as Julia Cameron says, you never know, you might find your "vein of gold", the one type of role (or genre of writing or style of painting or design) that fits you best, that brings out your personality and ability and talent the best. You never know what you can achieve, given consistency of effort and time. So *keep on truckin'*.

41

LETTER TO AN ASPIRING AUTHOR

*A*lthough the title of this chapter is "Letter to an aspiring author", it's really a letter to myself when I was younger, and desperately wanted to be an author and had no idea how to go about it, or whether I would ever fulfill that particular dream.

So here goes:

DEAR YOUNGER SELF (and Aspiring Author),

You probably want some advice on how to cross this bridge, which probably seems more like a chasm to you, from this side of not having written anything worth publishing, or having been published in some form that is deeply meaningful to you, to the other side of being able to call yourself "published author". You are desperate to put your feet on that side of the meadow, smell the flowers and feel the breeze in your hair.

You probably think that something magical will happen to you when you're over there. Somehow you will be anointed with some special oil. Music will play, and a banner will unfurl from the sky - You are now an author! You have made it!

Well, I am really sorry to burst your bubble, but it's not quite like that actually.

It is both easier and harder than you anticipated - being an author. In some ways, you are probably pursuing the wrong dream. I mean, it might work out for you. This dream, of being anointed and carried through the town on the shoulders of the masses, chanting your name. You might be that one in a million, whose books are read by your aunt's hairdresser and the husband of your child's pre-school teacher. You might fulfill that dream of reading your work to a packed auditorium, where there is a hush after you finish reading, and then the audience bursts out clapping at the sheer brilliance of your prose.

But I hope you realize that this doesn't happen to everyone who publishes a book. That there is a wide range between having written a book that is then bought by readers, to being bought and adored by hundreds of thousands. And that many wonderful writers and books are in the middle of this range. And if you are really serious about your love for words, you will not care where you are in the range at all, as long as you are there - that is, that your work is out there for readers to find and fall in love with, in the tens and dozens at least, if not thousands.

That doesn't mean that you shouldn't hope for the whole thing - the book tours, the adoration, the bestseller lists. It just means that this version of the dream is not the same thing as being a published author. It is just one version, one end of the spectrum. And here's the easy part - if you look closer, the dream is much bigger and more nuanced than you at first realized. There is room for you no matter what you want to write, and how wide or narrow the size of your potential readership is. You could write that space-vampire-fashionista novel that you have been imagining, or write another cozy mystery solved by a middle-aged spinster and her cat. There is enough room for your unique voice, your unique take, without you having to worry about trends, what's selling, what's hot, what is so over or over-saturated. If you love something, chances are someone else will too. If your dream is to write what's in your heart, and find someone who shares that interest, then being a published author, that's really not such an impossible dream. In fact, you're really lucky, because in the future things will change so much that anyone can write a book and become a published author.

And that was the good news. Now here is the bad: It is much harder than you have been led to believe. But not for the reasons you thought. You believed that you needed talent, great ideas, the whisper of the muse. You bought into the myth of writer's block, and searched for books and advice on combating it. You agonized over the smallest details of your story, before you had even written a single word. You worried about the correct spelling of the name of your main character, but neglected to worry about whether you liked her enough to spend a few months getting to know her on the page.

You talked more about the writing than you spent time on it. And when you did sit down to write, you realized the words didn't flow onto the page. You were appalled at the clunky and creaky sentences that dribbled from your fingers, and ground to a halt. You couldn't write this badly. Not if you wanted to be a published author. Not if you wanted those awards and accolades and book tours. So you stopped. Stopped writing. Stopped trying. Waited instead for the muse. Scribbled your ideas on scraps of paper. Carried around a notebook. Talked about the magnum opus you were going to write. When the circumstances were ideal. Which unfortunately never happened.

Here's what I want to tell you: write a shitty first draft. And shitty first book. And second and third. Write a lot of really bad blog posts. Give yourself permission to really suck for a year or two. It's not your fault. You're not a bad writer. You're not lacking in talent. You're simply lacking in skill. No one is born a writer, at least none of us mere mortals. Even that brilliant idea for a story that you have rattling around needs skill to bring it to life. Skill that you don't have just yet, skill that you have to work hard to acquire. And there really is only one way to acquire that skill. Write. Whether or not the muse flies by on her chariot. Whether or not the words you write make any sense. Whether or not you are in the mood.

Writer's block exists. Most of the time it is just another name for lack of experience. Of not knowing that the good words flow once you've written some bad ones down. Of not believing that you can edit out a lot of the clunkiness of your prose. Of not trusting that eventually the years of reading good books and soaking in the words will pay off.

So that's where I want to leave you, dear aspiring author. The hardest part of crossing that bridge to the meadow of "published author" isn't overcoming the obstacles you thought you would encounter. It is learning the craft, putting in the work and accepting that you might have to alter your definition of what being published means. But just in case all of this makes you feel just a little dampened and deflated, I want to assure you that the grass is still plenty green over there, the flowers are beautiful and little bunny rabbits occasionally scamper across. The reality of being published may differ from the vision in your head, and it might be more work, less glamorous, less dependent on luck and more on perseverance, but at the end, *it is worth it*.

And it gets a little easier, each time, with each book. And just a little harder too, just to keep you on your toes. After all, that's the price of admission.

ABOUT THE AUTHOR

Geetanjali Mukherjee grew up in India, spending her early years in Kolkata, and then attending high school in New Delhi. She went on to read law as an undergraduate at the University of Warwick, United Kingdom, where she joined as many clubs as possible while still giving the impression that she understood the intricacies of trusts law. She went on to earn a Master's degree in Public Administration from Cornell University, United States, while trying not to freeze along with the famed Ithaca lakes. She is also a member of Pi Alpha Alpha, the Global Honor Society for Public Affairs and Administration.

Geetanjali is the author of twelve books, although sometimes it feels like the one she is writing is the very first. She currently lives in Singapore.

Thank you for taking the time to read this book. I hope that it helps you on your writing journey, whether as a guiding light or a warm fire by which to rest for a while. I would love to hear from you about your writing projects and your journey as a working writer. Write to me: geetanjalimukherjee.author@ gmail.com or message me on social media.

facebook.com/geetumuk
instagram.com/geetumuk
threads.com/@geetumuk

ALSO BY GEETANJALI MUKHERJEE

- *Seamus Heaney: Select Poems*
- *From Auden to Yeats: Critical Analysis of 30 Selected Poems*
- *Illusions: A Collection of Poems*
- *Creating Consensus: The Journey Towards Banning Cluster Munitions*
- *Will The Real Albert Speer Please Stand Up? The Many Faces of Hitler's Architect*
- *Goldilocks Lives in Leamington: and Other Tales of University Life*
- *Negotiate, Persuade and Create Great Deals (co-authored with Michael Benoliel and Jose Yong)*

The Smarter Student Series

- *Anyone Can Get An A+: How To Beat Procrastination, Reduce Stress and Improve Your Grades*
- *Anyone Can Get An A+ Companion Workbook: How To Beat Procrastination, Reduce Stress and Improve Your Grades*
- *Acing Standardized Tests: How to Study Smart, Reduce Stress and Improve Your Test Score*

The Complete Writer Series

- *The Beginner Writer: How To Write - and Finish - Your First Book*
- *The Beginner Writer Workbook: How To Write - and Finish - Your First Book*

SAMPLE EXCERPT

The Beginner Writer

Chapter 1: Ideas Are Everywhere

Ideas are in the air, waiting to be captured.

Invariably if you read an interview with a writer or attend a book signing, someone will ask the question: "Where do you get your ideas?" Children's author R L Stine said recently that he has been asked some version of this question at every media interview. His answer: "The Idea Store". I imagine that, much like The Container Store, this is a store with a giant catalogue filled with all kinds of ideas for all kinds of situations, just waiting for you to pick one off a shelf. If only.

As a creative person, this question has always mystified me because I have always had ideas. Ideas to me are everywhere, they are simply waiting to be acted on. Therefore, I think the question is not simply about where to get ideas, but speaks more deeply to the belief about what constitutes an idea and its importance to the creative process.

From reading interviews with authors, it seems to me that for many authors, the idea for a book starts out just as a wisp – something small and intangible that just comes into one's mind as a question – what if? What if I were to write a book about shoes? Maybe shoes in the 18th century? Maybe write about shoes as they have evolved over time?

This idea is just a vague notion at first, but depending on your unique perspective it could develop in many ways – it could focus on the shoes of the aristocracy or shoes made by European fashion houses or on traditional shoes in Asia. You could write a novel about a shoemaker or a woman whose shoe-collection is out of control. There are so many ways and directions in which to take this simple germ of an idea.

Sometimes ideas come more fully formed. The idea for *Goldilocks Lives in Leamington,* my book of humorous essays, came from my mom, several years ago. At the time I didn't think I could write that book or even want to, but I filed the idea away. And many years later, it re-surfaced one day when it seemed like the right time to work on it. The final book did not differ much from the initial idea, which was to write stories about my experiences in college in the UK as an international student, particularly focusing on the incongruous situations I often found myself in.

At other times, the idea is simply a starting point. I wrote a short story for which the inspiration came to me a year or so earlier, while walking into my apartment building. In my mind, I saw a man taking the elevator to his apartment, shoulders slouched, dreading going home, because he had been keeping a secret from his wife and knew that he had to tell her today. All I knew at the time was what the secret was, but I knew nothing else. I had a clear picture of this man, but not his wife or the rest of the story. As I wrote, the details emerged, and in some ways surprised me. Even though the initial idea was only a partial one, by the time I sat down to write it, the rest of the story came to me.

I think those new to the field of writing or those who have not started writing regularly yet are quite nervous about how to get ideas. One question that all successful authors inevitably get asked is "Where do you get your ideas?" Other than tongue-in-cheek responses such as "The Idea Store, of course", authors invariably all say the same thing – ideas are everywhere. We simply have to notice them.

I think we also feel like we want to have big ideas – like the ideas for the Harry Potter series or the Hunger Games books. The once-in-a-generation amazing idea that blows people away. Those kinds of ideas probably are not just hanging about in the air waiting to be captured. On the other hand, if you look closely at the biographies of the authors of those books, they had the background knowledge to write what they did. The idea came to them as a mash-up or continuation of their own unique perspectives and interests.

For instance, I read in an interview that Suzanne Collins, the author of the Hunger Games trilogy, had grown up reading about Roman gladiators and Greek mythology, and added those layers to the story. Similarly, JK Rowling used her study of classical Latin and Greek to help inform many aspects of the Harry Potter series, not least the names of spells and creatures in the beloved books. While the ideas for both series are arguably exceptional, in both instances they came not quite from thin air, but were influenced by the authors' pre-existing influences and passions.

Read Voraciously

The most foolproof method I have found for getting ideas is simply to read, a lot, and in a wide array of genres. You never know what subject that you usually never look into or do not know a lot about will spark something. I believe that the best source of ideas comes simply from reading more widely. If you read the same things that everyone else reads, you will form the same opinions. And that isn't very interesting, is it? Someone will want to read your book because it is different from what else is out there, because it has your unique fingerprint. The more you read, particularly in different fields, the more unique your ideas and the expression of those ideas will be.

Reading within your genre can spark ideas to help with the story or its structure. For instance, if your thriller novel is flagging or reads a bit flat, reading some of the best examples in the genre might give rise to suggestions in your mind – what if the best friend gets kidnapped here? Or what if the main character is nearly killed in chapter 20? Similarly, reading other successful non-fiction books in your genre might help you to see ways to improve your own book – maybe by adding more examples to illustrate the theory, or bolstering the theoretical framework to add gravitas to your advice.

In general, reading the best examples of the genre you want to write in will elevate your own writing and improve your book tremendously. If you are writing a business book, read a wide variety of business books, both on your topic and in general – to get an idea of the market. There are many different kinds of business books, ranging from huge tomes that can double as doorstops to slim volumes sold at airport bookshops. Some are full of examples while others are stuffed with theory. Some have interviews with successful business founders, while others collate wisdom found from a variety of sources. Only by reading widely within your genre will you be able to figure out exactly what you want to write, for what sort of audience, in what style, and equally importantly, what you want to avoid.

The same goes for writing a memoir: you should read some of the most popular memoirs as well as some offbeat, non-main-stream ones. The more you read, the better sense you will have of the conventions of the genre, and what tools writers have used to present their story, how they have sustained the interest of the reader and what aspects worked and equally, did not work. As you read, you will get a better feel of what tone and style will work best for your own book.

Reading other authors does not mean that you copy their style or structure or even their content. The idea is not to plagiarize or steal from others, but to help you get a sense of what speaks to you, and strengthen your own style and voice. If you read only one other book on a subject and copy everything from it, you will be essentially reproducing a poor-quality version of that book. But if you read widely on the subject and around it, you will be drawing on a number of ideas and putting it together in your own unique way, through the lens of your own perspective. That will make your own work richer.

Reading outside your genre can be incredibly helpful as well, although in other ways. It is often said that creativity comes from two unrelated subjects colliding. You bring in ideas from one field and mash them up with ideas from an unrelated subject. The hit musical *Hamilton* is about American history but told through the medium of hip hop in a musical format.

Those two ideas were never combined in quite that way before. And it resulted in one of the most successful musicals of our time. Exposing yourself to new ideas in different genres and subjects will increase the likelihood that you find a unique and fresh idea.

Sometimes Ideas Find You

In her brilliant book on creativity, *Big Magic*, Elizabeth Gilbert writes that ideas are looking for a home just as much as we are looking for them. And sometimes *they* find *us*. But in order for that to happen, we have to be open to them. We have to be alert, and willing to listen and willing to be the right vessel to bring that idea to the world.

I have found that ideas can come to me at the strangest times, just when I am not expecting them. Often they appear when I am out for a walk, or sitting alone in a coffee shop or on public transport. Occasionally I get ideas while I am at work, when I scramble to reach for a pen to jot it down before I forget it. A lot of the times I don't write my ideas down at all, because they are a vague wisp. Sometimes the same idea keeps coming back over and over, in a slightly different and more fleshed out form. This is usually an indication that it is something I should pursue.

Famous writers in history have similarly reported having flashes out of nowhere with their idea. J K Rowling imagined the entire Harry Potter series on a train. J R R Tolkein wrote the first sentence of *The Hobbit* in a flash of inspiration while grading college papers. Stephen King attributes many of his story ideas to dreams: He got the idea for his novel *Misery* from a vivid dream in which a woman held a writer prisoner and killed him.

Many writers base characters and stories on people they know and settings that they are intimately familiar with. Mark Twain based Huckleberry Finn on his childhood friend. Director Mira Nair's film *Monsoon Wedding* was based on her and the writer Sabrina Dhawan's experiences growing up in India. I have often had ideas for stories and characters from people I met in passing or observed at a café or even neighbors and friends.

The best ideas also come from the essence of who you are. I think the kind of ideas that would come to Neil Gaiman would be different than the ones that would come to me. Even if we both heard the same intriguing line of overheard dialogue, or saw the same interesting exchange, we would have different ideas of how to turn that into a story. I think the ideas you come up with are based on your unique worldview - the kind of books you read, the people you meet, the places you have lived and the experiences you have had. If I really think about what the books I have written have in common – it's me. The ideas I pursued have come from things I have experienced, my interests, stories I have heard from people and books that have particularly influenced me.

Most of my books stem from my own specific interests and passions. I wrote a book on Albert Speer which was based on research I conducted during my Master's degree, as was my book on cluster munitions. I wrote a series of books for students because I struggled with my grades in high school for a while, before turning it around and receiving the highest grades in my year.

Sometimes you may also decide to write a book based on your expertise or knowledge about a particular subject. The genesis of this book came from questions people asked me about being a writer and how they too could write a book.

Even when the idea is not from my own life, my past and experiences influence what I notice. Recently I sat in a café and looked at three people sitting at a table and started imagining why they were all meeting there. I gave them a story in my head. Many writers do this – observe people in their surroundings, try to eavesdrop or just make up stories for people. But what made me choose this particular group and not any other? The tables at the café were full of people – but I focused on this group for some reason. And that's why each writer will get unique ideas, because even when they are observing the world, they are doing it with their own particular lens and perspective.

So if you are looking to get ideas, look no further than yourself. Ideas will come to you from who you are and your own life experience.

Ideas also tend to be shy and quiet. Sometimes we don't hear them unless we give them our full attention. Make space in your life for boredom. Make space for quiet contemplation. Go for walks alone (without listening to music or a podcast). Sit in public transport or a restaurant and just look at people, observe the world around you. When you attend an event or even a family gathering, see how people interact. Notice what people are not saying, or when their expressions and their words don't match up. Ideas can come to you at any moment – you just need to be paying attention.

An excerpt from The Beginner Writer: How To Write - And Finish - Your First Book. *Available in ebook and print.*